PRAISE FOR
Cherish

Cherish is full of wisdom, practical ad[...]
personal and sacred—how to live the ma[...]
Gary Thomas brings truth and reminds us of Jesus in the midst of our
earthly relationships.

JENNIE ALLEN, author of *Nothing to Prove*
and founder of IF:GATHERING

Many of us vowed "to love and to cherish" when we married. We hear
a lot of good advice about loving our spouses, and that's certainly
important—but there's more. Gary Thomas shows us how to put love
into action through cherishing the one we love.

JIM DALY, president of Focus on the Family

Gary Thomas has given a deep understanding and application of a key
biblical concept that is sure to take any married couple who applies
it to the next level. A must-read for every couple who wishes to grow
their relationship.

DR. TONY EVANS, president of The Urban Alternative

Sacred Marriage has become a classic, must-read book. Now Gary Thomas
has written another wonderful book, *Cherish*, that focuses not just on loving your spouse, but on cherishing—treasuring, honoring, holding dear
with tenderness, protecting, nurturing, and wanting to showcase—your
spouse. This must-read book will be a tremendous help and blessing to
couples and their marriages.

SIANG-YANG TAN, PhD, professor of psychology at
Fuller Theological Seminary, and author of *Counseling
and Psychotherapy: A Christian Perspective*

Two words come to mind every time I pick up a book by Gary Thomas: *profound* and *practical*. I often cover relationships on my radio show, and nobody articulates God's deepest desire for our relationships quite like Gary Thomas does. He's both convicting and encouraging, challenging and empowering. If your marriage feels dull and lackluster, read thoughtfully and prayerfully through Gary's new book, *Cherish*. You're only pages away from a new day and a new way of relating to your spouse.

SUSIE LARSON, talk radio host, national speaker, and author of *Your Powerful Prayers*

Every married person desires to love and cherish their spouse. Most of us have a sense of what it means to love well. Few of us have a vision of what it means to cherish our spouse. Gary Thomas paints a vivid picture of what it means to truly cherish another human being. This book reveals new pathways to grow a healthy, dynamic, and life-giving marriage.

DR. KEVIN G. HARNEY, pastor, author, and founder of Organic Outreach International.

There is nothing more beautiful than to be in a relationship with someone who is supposed to love you . . . and they actually love you. *Cherish* helps bring home that sweet, happy spot in marriage.

DR. TIM CLINTON, president of American Association of Christian Counselors

Get ready to be inspired! This book is sure to lift your marriage to a higher level—that's what it did for us. But Gary does more than inspire. He equips. He shows us how to lovingly care for and treasure our spouse like never before. Don't miss out on this incredibly practical message. Your marriage will never be the same.

DRS. LES & LESLIE PARROTT, #1 *New York Times* bestselling authors of *Saving Your Marriage Before It Starts*

Gary Thomas has done it again! He has a way of shifting my marriage paradigm to shed brilliant light on what it means practically to honor God in my marriage. By bringing to life one little word, *Cherish* will do the same for you.

Dr. Juli Slattery, president of Authentic Intimacy

Every couple gets married with great intentions for their marriage. Their marriage is going to be different; it's going to be special. But many couples lose their purpose, and life gets busy, hardships come, and the marriage they have isn't the marriage they wanted. Every couple wants to improve their marriage, but many don't know where to start. That's what I love about *Cherish*. Gary Thomas gets to the heart of marriage. Soak in his wisdom, apply these principles, and watch God transform your marriage relationship into something you cherish.

Justin Davis, pastor of Hope City Church, founder of RefineUs Ministries, and author of *Beyond Ordinary: When a Good Marriage Just Isn't Good Enough*

I've always been a huge fan of Gary Thomas's books, but *Cherish* is special. It shows couples how to turn disappointing marriages into delightful ones. I especially appreciated the chapter on honoring each other. As I work with couples in not just disappointing marriages but destructive ones, dishonoring is a significant issue. I'm grateful for Gary's validation of the fact that regularly withholding cherish in one's marriage can rise to the level of emotional abuse.

Leslie Vernick, licensed counselor, relationship coach, and author of the bestselling *The Emotionally Destructive Relationship*

Also by Gary Thomas

Authentic Faith
Devotions for a Sacred Marriage
Devotions for Sacred Parenting
Every Body Matters
The Glorious Pursuit
Holy Available (previously titled *The Beautiful Fight*)
A Lifelong Love
Not the End but the Road
Pure Pleasure
Sacred Influence
Sacred Marriage
Sacred Parenting
Sacred Pathways
The Sacred Search
Thirsting for God

Cherish

The One Word that Changes Everything for Your Marriage

GARY THOMAS

ZONDERVAN

Cherish
Copyright © 2017 by Gary Thomas

Requests for information should be addressed to:
Zondervan, *3900 Sparks Dr. SE, Grand Rapids, Michigan 49546*

ISBN 978-0-310-34729-3 (international trade paper edition)
ISBN 978-0-310-34727-9 (ebook)

Library of Congress Cataloging-in-Publication Data

> **Names:** Thomas, Gary (Gary Lee), author.
> **Title:** Cherish : the one word that changes everything for your marriage / Gary Thomas.
> **Description:** Grand Rapids: Zondervan, 2017. | Includes bibliographical references.
> **Identifiers:** LCCN 2016020845 | ISBN 9780310347262 (hardcover)
> **Subjects:** LCSH: Marriage—Religious aspects—Christianity.
> **Classification:** LCC BV835 .T468 2017 | DCC 248.8/44—dc23 LC record available at
> https://lcnn.loc.gov/2016020845

Published in association with Yates & Yates, www.yates2.com.

Cover design: James W. Hall IV
Interior design: Denise Froehlich

First Printing November 2016 / Printed by CPI Group (UK) Ltd, Croydon CR0 4YY

To Skip and Lucy

Contents

Acknowledgments

I t may sound weird to say this upfront in the acknowledgments, but from the landing of the idea to the daily process of writing, God has felt like an ever-present partner in this book. On days when I needed an illustration for one specific point, a couple "just happened" to recount the perfect illustration during a spontaneous meeting. Many days of writing felt like straight-out worship. I am enormously grateful to serve a living God who I believe is eager to see his church grow. To say "I couldn't have written this book without him" would be the understatement of my life. To me, at least, it felt like God was all over it.

Many thanks to Brooks Powell, Mary Kay Smith, Alli Smith, and my wife, Lisa, for previewing earlier incarnations of this manuscript.

I am very grateful for the many friends and readers who graciously shared their own stories. Some have had details changed to protect their privacy; many allowed their lives to be shared unaltered. This book is a collection of the life experience of Jesus at work in marriages and the church.

My editor, John Sloan, pushed me pretty hard on this one, for which I am very grateful; his work has made this a much better book. I am grateful to the entire Zondervan team: David Morris, the publisher, has been an active and enthusiastic advocate. Tom Dean, my marketing director, has been patient and tireless, and Brandon Henderson and Robin Barnett have provided outstanding marketing and public relations support. Dirk Buursma's faithfulness in copyediting sets the standard for the rest of the publishing world.

I couldn't imagine being a part of this ministry without my agents, Curtis Yates and Mike Salisbury, by my side with their guidance, counsel, and advocacy.

One of the things that has given me freedom to focus on writing is having children who follow the Lord and make great choices. My son, Graham, and his wife, Molly, inspire me with their love. Allison and Kelsey are a daily delight. I've seen so many parents weighed down with anxiety over their children that I feel particularly blessed to be inspired by these four amazing young adults.

And as always, I feel blessed beyond measure by the support I receive and the community I experience in Houston, Texas, that goes by the name of Second Baptist Church, and my wife, Lisa, who has taught me the joys of cherishing and being cherished every day.

Foreword

BY LISA THOMAS

I know what it feels like to be cherished.

A warm hand covering my cheek, maybe with a little eye contact

A gentle back rub

A cup of coffee by my bedside when I wake up in a hotel room

Words of affirmation, beyond what I deserve, sometimes even spoken in a room full of strangers

A hand pressed on the small of my back

A gas tank that remains miraculously full

Soft words when a harsh response might have been justifiable

Some of these things might make *you* feel annoyed rather than cherished! Cherishing takes on different forms for each of us, but for me, it is the little acts that leave me feeling adored, safe, worth the effort. Just hearing the word *cherish* makes me want to hug Gary, give him a kiss on the cheek, and say thank you.

My friend asked me recently what book Gary was working on. I told her it was a new marriage book called *Cherish*. She instinctively grabbed her husband's arm, leaned into him, and let out a delighted "aaah." Just the word elicited that response. I am confident this book, written by one who excels at cherishing, will help you learn to cherish well.

CHAPTER 1

To Love and to Cherish

A cherishing attitude will
enrich, deepen, and spiritually
strengthen your marriage

Khanittha "Mint" Phasaeng's life changed dramatically in 2015 when she was crowned a Thai beauty queen. Her pageant win, according to the *Daily Mail*, led to lucrative film, advertising, and television contracts. Shortly after returning to her hometown, Mint became an Internet sensation when she was photographed showing honor to her trash-collecting mother by kneeling at her feet.

Mint's mother literally collects and sells trash for a living, so that's why Mint found her in front of trash bins when she returned from her triumphant win—still dressed in the tiara and colorful sash that marked her as one of Thailand's new celebrities.

The photo of a glamorous young woman kneeling on the dirty pavement in front of a trash collector wearing plastic shoes evokes a wondrous gasp. Without shame, Mint called her mother's trade an "honorable profession" that kept their family from starvation, and she praised her mother's commitment and care.

One week before Mint's win, her mother was all but invisible to 99.999 percent of Thailand. But when she was cherished by a suddenly famous daughter, millions got to hear her story and learn of her character and her worth.

This is a picture of what happens when we cherish a loved one. Mint didn't just send her mother a thank-you card. She didn't just give her mother a halfhearted hug. She got her dress dirty as she dropped to her knees in a place where people throw their garbage and bowed down to a woman in common dress.

This sign of respect, adoration, gratitude, and honor—going out of your way to notice someone, appreciate someone, honor someone, hold someone dear—in such a visible way, even kneeling at their feet, is a picture of what we could call "cherish." Mint felt something in her heart, believed something in her mind, and expressed something physically by dropping to her knees.

She cherished her mother.

Ever notice how our attention is drawn to something whenever we see that it is given special care? When you're walking around Washington, D.C., and a police motorcade of black SUVs escorts a car with tiny United States flags on it, you know the person inside must be important.

They're being protected, after all.

You don't put a Tiffany engagement ring in a shoebox. You don't frame a Rembrandt in a Popsicle stick frame. You wouldn't use a genuine George Washington autograph as a coaster.

The way we treat something acknowledges whether we cherish it or hold it with indifference or contempt. To truly cherish something is to go out of our way to show it off, protect it, and honor it. We want others to see and recognize and affirm the value that we see.

Just as an art collector will survey many frames and attempt many different lighting angles and then consider many different walls on which to showcase a particularly valuable piece of art, so when we cherish a person, we will put time, thought, and effort into honoring, showcasing, and protecting them.

Cultivating a cherishing attitude toward your spouse will elevate your marriage relationally, emotionally, spiritually, and even physically. You will set different goals for your relationship. You will look at your marriage from entirely different angles. While cherish may seem to start out as an internal reality, it will always be reflected *by what you do*, and it can revolutionize your marriage.

The Neglected Word

Millions of couples getting married have pledged "to love and to cherish, till death do us part."

Most of us understand and get the love part—commitment, putting the other person first, service—but what does it mean to cherish our spouses? Is that word just an add-on? Why do we say it once at the wedding and then rarely even mention it again?

Exploring and understanding what it means to cherish each other will enrich, deepen, and spiritually strengthen our marriages. Cherish isn't just a throwaway word, but an idea that helps us better understand what we are called to do and to be in marriage. Learning to truly cherish each other turns marriage from an obligation into a delight. It lifts marriage above a commitment to a precious priority.

Cherish is the melody that makes a marriage sing.

Sadly, the word *cherish* is more popularly used for things and memories than it is for people, but such common uses can help us understand what the word means. To cherish something means we want to *protect* it (you don't leave a $100,000 Mercedes out in the street with the door open and the keys in it), *honor* it ("come and see the new car I got!"), *treat* it *with tenderness* (avoiding streets filled with potholes), *nurture* it (oil changes and tune-ups), and go out of our way to *indulge* it (frequent washes and wax jobs).

To cherish something is to *hold it dear.* That means you think about it, and when you do, you feel great pleasure. You have great affection for it.

If you cherish something, you go out of your way to show it is important to you and thus you *showcase* it. How many times does a newly engaged woman show off her engagement ring to friends and coworkers? How many times does an excited new car owner ask his friends to come outside and see his new "baby"?

Applied to relationships, when we cherish someone, we naturally want to *protect* them—it could be physical protection, but also protection of an emotional or spiritual sort, or their reputation or health. We'll *treat them with tenderness*, because they matter so much to us. We will look for ways to *nurture* them and at least occasionally go out of our way to *indulge* them. If we cherish someone, we will *hold them dear.* That means we will purposely think about them, and when we do, it will bring us great pleasure. The thought of them will make us smile. When we cultivate such an affection toward someone, we naturally want others to see their worth so we find ways to *showcase* our spouses to others, so others can take the same pleasure from our spouses' excellence as we do.

In one sense, love is the nurturing aspect of marriage, while cherish is the "tasting" aspect of marriage. Love meets the need; cherish tickles the tongue.

"She Is So Cherish"

The urban dictionary uses the word *cherish* to describe someone who is unbelievably amazing: "She is so cherish!"

That sentence—"She is so cherish!"—is the style in which Song of Songs is written. Indeed, as love is known by 1 Corinthians 13, so cherish is captured in Song of Songs.

- Love is about being gracious and altruistic.

   "Love is patient, love is kind" (1 Corinthians 13:4).

- Cherish is about being enthusiastic and enthralled.

   *"How much more pleasing is your love than
   wine, and the fragrance of your perfume more
   than any spice"* (Song of Songs 4:10).

- Love tends to be quiet and understated.

   *"[Love] does not envy, it does not
   boast"* (1 Corinthians 13:4).

- Cherish boasts boldly and loudly.

   *"My beloved is radiant and ruddy, outstanding
   among ten thousand"* (Song of Songs 5:10).

- Love thinks about others with selflessness.

   *"[Love] is not proud. It does not dishonor others,
   it is not self-seeking"* (1 Corinthians 13:4–5).

- Cherish thinks about its beloved with praise.

    *"Your voice is sweet, and your face is
    lovely"* (Song of Songs 2:14).

- Love doesn't want the worst for someone.

    "Love does not delight in evil" (1 Corinthians 13:6).

- Cherish celebrates the best in someone.

    *"How beautiful you are, my darling! Oh,
    how beautiful!"* (Song of Songs 1:15).

- Love puts up with a lot.

    "[Love] always hopes, always perseveres"
    (1 Corinthians 13:7).

- Cherish enjoys a lot.

    *"His mouth is sweetness itself; he is altogether
    lovely"* (Song of Songs 5:16).

- Love is about commitment.

    *"Love . . . endures all things. Love never
    ends"* (1 Corinthians 13:7–8 ESV).

- Cherish is about delight and passion.

    *"Your name is like perfume poured
    out"* (Song of Songs 1:3).

Love and cherish never compete—they complement each other and even complete each other. At times, they certainly overlap. By pursuing cherish, we'll become better lovers as well.

Men, your wives don't want you to just "love" them in the sense of being committed to them; they want you to cherish them. They don't want us to stop at, "I will be committed to you and never leave you"; they want to hear:

- "Like a lily among thorns is my darling among the young women" (Song of Songs 2:2).
- "You are altogether beautiful, my darling; there is no flaw in you" (Song of Songs 4:7).
- "You have stolen my heart, my sister, my bride; you have stolen my heart with one glance of your eyes" (Song of Songs 4:9).

And women, you'll discover that a cherished husband is the happiest of husbands. A friend of mine asked seven male friends, "Do your wives love you?" and every one of them answered yes. He then asked, "Do your wives like you?" and every one answered no.

All seven husbands feel *loved*, but none feel *cherished*.

Husbands want to hear their wives say, "Like an apple tree among the trees of the forest is my beloved among the young men" (Song of Songs 2:3).

Cherishing your husband will motivate you to pursue him and thus raise the temperature of your marriage: "I will search for the one my heart loves" (Song of Songs 3:2).

Cherishing your husband will help you dwell on his most excellent qualities, giving you greater satisfaction in marriage: "His mouth is sweetness itself; he is altogether lovely. This is my beloved, this is my friend" (Song of Songs 5:16).

The good news is that cherishing your spouse is something you can learn to do. It's not just a feeling that comes and goes; there are spiritual and relational practices that generate feelings of cherishing your spouse as you act on them so you *do* hold them dear in your heart. Learning to cherish actually *creates* joy, fulfillment, happiness, and satisfaction. It's one of those spiritual realities that may not make logical sense, but when you take it by faith and put it into practice, it works.

It just does.

Learning to take our marriage from polite coexisting or even just basic friendship to the much higher spiritual call of learning to truly cherish each other is what this book is all about. It's a spiritual journey before it's a marital journey. God's Word will instruct us; we'll need his Spirit to empower us and his truth to enlighten us to shape our hearts in such a way that we are able to cherish those who "stumble in many ways" (James 3:2), even as God cherishes us as we stumble in many ways. If you believe your marriage has all but died or even just gotten a little stale, the hope behind learning to cherish each other in marriage is found in this: *God is more than capable of teaching us and empowering us to treat and cherish our spouses the way he treats and cherishes us.*

You've been challenged to love in many marriage books. This book will challenge you to cherish, which will take your love to an entirely new level. Through the biblical act of cherishing, we can empower our spouses to become who they are called by God to be, and in the process to become more of who we are called to be, creating a marriage that feels more precious, more connected, and more satisfying.

I am not in any way diminishing love as the main qualifier of a biblical marriage. Love will always be the backbone of biblical relationships. But studying cherish, with its special qualities, puts a polish on love, makes it shine, and thus adds a special sparkle to our life and marriage.

A Higher Vision

"Sometimes I feel guilty that we have it so good."

Jaclyn and Donnie have been married for eleven years. They own two businesses and have three daughters, ages ten and under.

The way these two cherish each other is infectious. I spoke to them on March 21, which they affectionately call "Jaclyn and Donnie Day" because it's the anniversary of their first date. They describe their marriage as "all about the dance." Because their kitchen is so small, they have to navigate with the precision of the Blue Angels at high speed, but somehow they still manage to get everything done in a small space without tripping over each other. "That's the best picture of our life together," Donnie says.

Both Jaclyn and Donnie are lastborns with "peacemaker personalities" (their words), and they go out of their way to stay connected. They never watch television alone—and that involves compromise. "If I have to watch *Nashville* with her, she watches *Agents of S.H.I.E.L.D.* with me," Donnie says. They don't want individual hobbies to pull them apart. In fact, they don't even let work pull them apart; they work out of the same office.

It's the way they are so in tune with each other that marks them as a "cherishing" couple. Donnie is a master at reading Jaclyn's mood and silently pouring her a glass of wine or bringing her a chunk of chocolate before things get critical with the kids or the work/life stress sours her mood. During fifteen-minute breaks while volunteering at a church service, they find each other. If they're walking next to each other, they're touching—holding hands or linking arms. Their language is intentional; several times a day they say, "You're my favorite. Can I keep you?" They protect each other and appreciate each other in ways you'll see described throughout this book, but I'm introducing them at the start so you can see that the kind of marriage I'm talking about is possible.

We need stories of couples who struggle, persevere, and come out on the other side; I recount a lot of those kinds of stories in *Sacred Marriage*. But we also need stories of couples who find the "sweet, happy spot" of marriage. Those are the marriages *Cherish* seeks to inspire.

There's a parallel in the art world. First-century Roman art is marked by its lifelike realism. In early Roman sculpture, the generals and women have real bodies and even, in many cases, wrinkles. The subjects might be bald, pockmarked, chubby, or short. That's because the sculptures depict real citizens with real images.

Greek sculpture from the same time period is more idealistic. Because the sculptures so frequently depict gods and athletes, they tend to be more exalted, trying to exhibit the ideal of ultimate fitness, chiseled strength, and perfect beauty.

My first book on marriage, *Sacred Marriage*, caused a bit of a stir by admitting and addressing the difficult realities of marriage—we looked into the wrinkles of marriage and the occasional ugly realities of relating as two sinners. *Sacred Marriage* was thus a "Roman" book. *Cherish: The One Word That Changes Everything for Your Marriage* is a bit more of a "Greek" book. We're looking at the ideal, knowing it is so wonderful that we may never achieve it fully, but believing that pursuing it leads us to a place so beautiful that the journey is well worth taking. Knowing that such a marriage exists inspires us to reach just a bit higher.

Sacred Marriage was about how God can use the difficulties inherent in every marriage for a good purpose. *Cherish* is about how God can give us hearts to delight in each other so we can enjoy a marriage where we sometimes even feel guilty because we have it so good.

Most of us don't want marriages where we grit our teeth and tolerate each other just because God's Word says we don't "qualify" for a divorce. Most of us don't want marriages where our spouses really don't like us, much less respect us. We want to be cherished, and we want to be married to someone we cherish. And I'm suggesting it's possible to get to that point if we want to, even if we've stopped cherishing each other.

Doesn't cherish seem more pleasant, enjoyable, and fulfilling than hatred, indifference, or mere tolerance? Why wouldn't we want to grow in cherishing each other? What keeps us from cherishing each other? What is the road back to learning how to cherish someone who has hurt us, disappointed us, frustrated us, and angered us? Can we look past that and still cherish an imperfect spouse?

Let's focus on this oft-forgotten second word in the marriage vows—what it means to cherish.

CHERISHING CHERISH

- In our marriage vows, we promise to love and cherish each other, so why do we talk so much about love and so little about cherish?

- Cherish means to go out of our way to notice someone, appreciate someone, honor someone, and hold someone dear.

- When we cherish someone, we take pleasure in thinking about them, and we want to showcase their excellence to others.

- In one sense, love is the nurturing aspect of marriage, while cherish is the "tasting" aspect of marriage. Love meets the need; cherish tickles the tongue.

- Love is celebrated in 1 Corinthians; cherish is showcased in Song of Songs.

- The theme of this book is this: through the biblical act of proper cherishing, we can empower our spouses to become who they are called by God to be, and in the process can see ourselves becoming more of who we are called to be, creating a marriage that feels more precious, more connected, and more satisfying.

- The God who cherishes the imperfect us can teach us and empower us to cherish our imperfect spouses.

QUESTIONS FOR DISCUSSION AND REFLECTION

1. Why do you think we talk so much about love and so little about cherish?

2. Describe a marriage where one or both partners practiced cherishing their spouse. What did it look like? How did it inspire you?

3. What struck you most about the contrast between love and cherish from 1 Corinthians and Song of Songs?

4. How does love help us understand cherish, and how does cherish help us understand love?

5. Describe a season in your relationship when you felt especially cherished. How did it affect the way you looked at yourself and your relationship?

CHAPTER 2

The Only Man/ Woman in the World

Cherish means learning to hold someone dear

Men, if you want superlative satisfaction in your marriage, if you would enjoy a love for your wife that has no compare, if you want to know what it truly means to cherish your wife, then go back with me to the beginning of time—when Adam walked the earth with God.

Learning to cherish our wives takes us all the way back to the garden of Eden.

Adam watched animals play, discovered a wide variety of plants, had trees to climb, and talked to a God who was beyond imagining.

But there was no one like him.

No one.

God then put Adam in a deep sleep. When Adam woke up, he could hardly believe his eyes. Before him stood Eve—like him in the most important ways, but also so unlike him in even more important ways.

Those lips! Eyes that seemed curiously softer. Legs like his, but somehow, gloriously different.

Breasts!

Curves from shoulder to feet that, to this day, still make men sigh.

And she was his, as he was hers.

What made this moment especially powerful, momentous, enthralling?

There was no Holly, Shanice, or Sofia.

There was just Eve.

Adam couldn't compare Eve's back to Camila's, or Eve's legs to Emma's. He couldn't say, "Eve is kinder than Janet," or "Eve isn't as intelligent as Claire," because there was only Eve in all her glory, the woman who defined "woman" to the first man. He couldn't imagine any other woman, because there wasn't one. He couldn't wonder what it would be like if she were taller or heavier or slimmer or darker or funnier or more intelligent.

She just was.

The only woman in the world.

And Adam couldn't have been happier.

If you want to be fully satisfied in your marriage, if you want your wife to feel cherished, then mentally treat your wife like Eve. Let her be, in your mind, in that way, the only woman in the world. Say with King Solomon, "My dove, my perfect one, is the only one" (Song of Songs 6:9 ESV).

Remember that day when your bride walked down the aisle and you lost your breath seeing your woman in all her glory, marching forward to give herself to you? No one else existed for you at that moment. No other woman came to mind. Everyone else was background furniture compared to the glorious bride who was about to become your wife.

I've stood next to many men in that moment—some of them breaking down and crying in front of family and coworkers.

This doesn't have to be a once-in-a-lifetime experience. It can be a daily reality.

To cherish our wives this way, we have to mentally choose to not look at any other woman that way. If you compare a two-carat diamond to a three-carat diamond, it will look small in comparison, even though it's bigger and more expensive than 99 percent of the wedding ring diamonds out there. If you compare a comfortable three-thousand-square-foot home to a ten-thousand-square-foot mansion, the three-thousand-square-foot home may not feel so satisfying.

Pray a prayer that I refer to in *Sacred Marriage*, one I prayed early on in my own marriage: "Lord, let my wife define beautiful to me. Let her be the standard for what I find most attractive."

God has answered this prayer, and it's so affirming to my wife. However she is, is what I am most attracted to. She is the "plumb line" of beauty for me—a plumb line that ages with her.

It is stunning to me that recently, after thirty-one years of marriage, my wife was standing in front of me, feeling all stressed-out, talking about how tired she felt and how frustrating certain aspects of her day had been. While trying to respond with empathy on the outside, inside I was thinking, "She is gorgeous. Still gorgeous."

We can't fill up our eyes with our wives if our eyes have been previously filled with someone else. One of the many dangers of porn is that it neurologically trains us to find our wives less beautiful.

I was working with a young husband who struggled in this area. After just a few weeks of victory, he saw his wife sitting across from him at a restaurant, and he started beaming.

"What?" his wife asked, noticing his intense delight.

"You're just so . . . *gorgeous* tonight."

She didn't yet know what I knew—his eyes had been retrained, and it was showing. He was almost giddy just talking about it.

He won, she won, and even God smiled, because that night his son was cherishing his daughter, just the way God designed marriage to work.

If I want to cherish my wife's body, I have to guard against building an attraction to any other body. That doesn't mean you can't find others attractive; it does define how you look at them and where you let your mind go.

It goes far beyond physical appearance, of course. I don't compare my wife's occasional frustrations with another woman's peace, just as I won't compare my wife's skill set to another woman's gifts. If I want supreme satisfaction in Lisa, if I want to truly *cherish* her, she must become to me like Eve, the only woman in the world. The only one I will ever look at in *that way*.

I defy any man to honestly say he has derived any lasting, godly satisfaction from looking at another woman the way he should look only at his wife; after the short moment of excitement, there will be a much longer season of frustration and discontent, followed by anger and marital distance. Fantasizing about another woman is the highway to discontent and marital distance. It never leads you to your wife; it carries you away from her at seventy miles an hour. That's how you create discontent, assault any attitude of cherishing your wife, and ruin your own happiness.

Adam was so blessed—and so happy, accordingly—because there was literally no one else to compare Eve to. And while the world is now populated with billions of other women, we men can still make the choice to look at our wives as Adam looked at Eve, the only woman who matters in that way.

To fill up our eyes with only her.

To be so taken with her that there is no Juliet, no Jada, and no Anna.

Just Eve.

It's a prayer first: "Lord, let me look at my wife as the only woman in the world."

Then it's a choice.

Then we guard our hearts and keep our focus.

It requires a recommitment when we stumble. We will have to go back and pray again. We will have to choose again.

But if we keep holding her dear, mentally reserving our focus exclusively for her, eventually it happens: our wives are cherished. Our wives aren't just our first choice, but our *only* choice.

We become happy, satisfied, fulfilled.

Because your wife defines beauty for you, your picture of the most beautiful woman in the world ages with your wife. You won't be a sixty-year-old man pining after a twenty-five-year-old model. Who wants to be that guy anyway?

You'll eventually be a sixty-year-old husband who is enthralled with his sixty-year-old wife and still finds his heart skipping a beat when she smiles in her own particular way or stands in front of you in that dress and the sun hits her just right and you forget about everything else, including time.

You've taught yourself to cherish her, and it's worked. You've become enthralled with her, as you are with no other woman.

You want this, men. Trust me. You do. It is one of the supreme blessings of marriage that is often overlooked.

Cherishing is about learning to hold our spouses dear, and this takes vigilance. It takes intention. It takes practice. But when it arrives—when your wife is Eve and there is no other— you will feel like the most blessed husband alive.

Your wife will feel cherished because your adoration will be as genuine as the beginning of time. Your heavenly Father will experience joy because he delights when his daughter is richly cherished. Your kids will feel secure because they spiritually feed off their parents' affection.

Everybody wins. Everybody.

But Adam wins the most.

The Only Man in the World

Women, may I invite you to take the same journey back to the garden of Eden, to the door of true happiness in marriage, and suggest that the key to that door, to becoming the most pleased and happiest of wives, is to begin viewing your husband as Adam, the only man in the world?

Divorce statistics and personal anecdotes reflect that women tend to be more dissatisfied in their marriages than men. You may have to fight fiercely against the onslaught of disappointment, lest you be tugged toward frustration, collapse into bitterness, and find yourself a captive to contempt.

How can you fight contempt? How can you learn to cherish your husband as if he were the only man on earth?

Here's the spiritual choice you have to make: when any woman gets married, she agrees—consciously or not—to a "commitment of contentment." She forever resets the boundaries for what makes her content. She doesn't get to compare her husband to other husbands (critically comparing is what girlfriends should do with boyfriends, not what wives should do with husbands) because to her, he must become the only man in the world. "I am my beloved's and my beloved is mine" (Song of Songs 6:3).

You've already made your choice. In your ideal world, you have no intention of ever starting over with someone else, so why not put your energy into and your focus on guarding that choice, building on the strengths of that choice, and making yourself ever more grateful that you made that choice? Think of yourself as Eve in the garden of Eden, standing before the first man, Adam. Eve didn't have anyone to compare Adam to. She couldn't think, *His arms look below average, but at least he doesn't have a unibrow.* All she could possibly think was, *This is what a man is like. This is what my man is like.*

If you don't do this, your husband will pick up on the fact that he's being compared. Men notice what you notice.

Brooks was a champion high school swimmer in his high school and state, so successful that he was offered and took an athletic position in Princeton's varsity swim program. His impressed girlfriend (who eventually became his wife) occasionally made an offhand remark when she saw a football player or a Hollywood type who was particularly "stacked," muscle-wise. Brooks thought that must be what Shelby wanted, so he focused more of his training on becoming stronger and stockier. The problem is that swimmers don't need the shoulders or chest of a bodybuilder. In fact, those things can make a swimmer less effective. So Brooks was inadvertently trying to become someone who would ultimately be less successful at what initially drew Shelby's attention.

Had Shelby known what Brooks was thinking, she would have been appalled. She wasn't expressing displeasure with Brooks's build when she admired other men; she was simply making offhand remarks without at all meaning to diminish her boyfriend's strengths.

Unfortunately, most men hear everything with hypersensitive ears. We notice when a woman's eyes light up, and we notice when they don't.

No man can be everything. A successful long-distance cyclist can't be a bodybuilder (the only people in the world I feel okay comparing my arms to are those who race in the Tour de France). A handyman may be able to fix a lot of things, but he may view exercise or long talks as chores rather than something he relishes. Though there are exceptions, dedicating one's time to becoming exceptional at one thing usually means not being exceptional at a whole lot of other things.

Since no one man can be everything, one of the best gifts a woman can give a man is to tell him—with her eyes, attention, words, and acceptance—"You don't have to be anything other than what you are. You are my Adam, the only man in the world. I cherish *you.*"

With such an attitude, anything your husband isn't becomes irrelevant—your guy isn't that, so you don't expect that, and there's no point in fretting over it. If you marry a guy who isn't a handyman, you don't judge him for not being a handyman. If you marry a guy who is a bit silent, you don't brood over the fact that your best friend's husband will sit and talk to her for hours. If you marry a guy who thinks exercise is picking up the video game controller, you don't think about what it would be like to marry a guy who does triathlons with you.

Instead, you think of your man as Adam—the only man in the world. You cherish him for what and who he is, don't expect him to be anything else, and never compare him to anyone else.

This may sound extreme to some of you, but tell me, what have you ever gained by comparing your husband's weaknesses to another husband's strengths? Has it ever made you happier or more contented in your marriage—or a more loving wife? Has it made you feel closer to your husband and given you more joy? Has it ever helped your husband become something he's not?

Of course not.

Many wives have complained to me about their husbands dealing with the stress of unemployment by escaping into video games for hours on end; I completely understand how frustrating this must be. And yet there are numerous wives whose husbands work very hard but disappoint their wives in other ways. The fact that they work hard is completely discounted, however. It's taken for granted. "That's what a man does."

Not all men, trust me. Not the ones playing eight hours of video games waiting for a potential employer to call.

The way our brains work is that we *tolerate* our spouse's strengths by assuming that's the bottom line, the ground floor, so if you married a superlative husband, to you he's just average and there are still so many ways he can disappoint you.

Some wives—if they were to wake up and find the bed

beside them empty because their husband had already left for work—would worship God for a full fifteen minutes.

Finally! He's working!

Other women wake up in an empty bed and think, *I hope he doesn't forget to pick up the dry cleaning on his way home like he did yesterday.*

At some point, if you want marital happiness, if you want to learn how to cherish a real man instead of longing for an imaginary composite, some "Frankenstein" husband who somehow has it all, then you have to own your choice and even learn to cherish your choice. "My vineyard, my very own, is for myself" (Song of Songs 8:12 NRSV).

I promise you that you will be so much happier in your marriage—you will become a much better wife—if you simply pray through the creation account in Genesis and begin thinking of your husband as Adam—the man who defines all other men for you—and then start treating him that way. It'll take biblical understanding, then prayerful supplication to God ("God, help me do this"), then an intellectual consent ("I want to do this"), and finally a determined act of the will ("I'm going to do this") to fully go through this process, resetting your brain to think of your husband as Adam.

Fight disappointment with biblical understanding—this book, I trust, will help you do that.

Fight frustration by asking God to give you gratitude for your man, to help you see your man as God does, as his son.

Fight bitterness with intellectual focus—you will think about his excellent qualities and talk to yourself about your husband's excellent qualities instead of listening to yourself fret over his inadequacies.

If you do that, contempt will slowly give way to cherish.

It's not a one-time deal. You'll catch yourself slipping back into comparison at times, and then you'll have to go back to square one and set the process in motion once again. Over time, it will just become the way you look at your husband. Thinking of him as Adam will be your default mode.

When that happens, you'll find that you cherish your husband instead of having contempt for him. You'll discover that you are grateful for his strengths instead of bitter about his weaknesses. You'll experience the joy of your heavenly Father, who delights in seeing his sons cherished, encouraged, and respected. You'll be a strong witness to Christians and non-Christians alike. You'll provide one of the best parenting role models a mother could ever provide for her children.

But just as importantly, you'll find more contentment, enjoyment, happiness, and intimacy in your marriage. Your heart will swell with pride, and you will be the envy of all your friends—the one woman in their circle who is utterly and contentedly in love with her husband and can't even imagine being married to any other.

That's a very pleasant place to live.

CHERISHING CHERISH

- To make our spouses feel cherished, and for our own happiness and satisfaction, we must view each other as Adam and Eve, the only man or woman in the world.

- Comparing our spouses' shortcomings to anyone else's strengths never increases marital satisfaction, never helps our spouses grow, and only discourages us. So we should just avoid doing it altogether.

- Men need to pray that God would make their wives the very definition of beauty. They should preserve and protect that special moment of being enthralled with their brides as they walked up the aisle on their wedding day, wanting that to be a daily reality. Comparison of any kind will kill this reality.

- Women frequently struggle with disappointment in marriage. Viewing their husbands as Adam will help them overcome this.

- Making a marital choice establishes a new "commitment to contentment." Once we make our choice about whom to marry, we have to own that choice, accept the consequences of that choice, and learn to build on the best aspects of that choice.

- Recognize that no one spouse can excel in everything; in fact, to excel in one area almost always requires making sacrifices in other areas.

- One of the best gifts we can give our spouses is to tell them with our words, affection, and eyes, "You don't have to be anyone other than who you are. You are my Eve/Adam, the only woman/man in the world to me."

QUESTIONS FOR
DISCUSSION AND REFLECTION

1. Viewing your spouse as Eve or Adam is one way of describing the act of fully accepting the choice you made when you got married. Talk about what it means mentally, emotionally, and spiritually to finally and fully accept this choice, build on this choice, and eventually even revel in this choice.

2. Fashion a prayer you can begin using, asking God to make your spouse the very definition of beauty. Discuss why this is a spiritually healthy thing to do and how it will help you cherish your spouse more.

3. Why do you think it is more common for women to struggle with marital dissatisfaction than men? How should both husbands and wives respond to this tendency?

4. Just for fun, invite the men to discuss the ideal "composite woman." Invite the women to talk about the ideal "composite man." Notice how some ideals will directly contradict each other. What do you think God is teaching us by pointing us toward learning how to cherish a real man and a real woman rather than a composite?

5. What can you do in the coming weeks to assure your spouse that he is your Adam or that she is your Eve, the only man or woman in the world?

CHAPTER 3

Marriage as Ballet

Cherishing means learning to showcase your spouse

Famed Russian-born ballet choreographer George Balanchine once said, "Ballet is woman."[1] The best male dancers recognize that their role is all about showcasing the female dancer's beauty, particularly during *pas de deux*—couples' dancing. People generally go to the ballet to see the beautiful form, grace, balance, coordination, and strength of the female lead, but all of those qualities are even better showcased when the ballerina has a male dancer who can set her up, catch her, and support her.

As a former male dancer and later choreographer, Balanchine said his job was to "make the beautiful more beautiful."[2]

With a strong and gifted male dancer nearby, the ballerina can do more and attempt more than she could in a solo endeavor. In the words of Sarah Jessica Parker (who put together a documentary on the New York City Ballet), "When a male dancer is paired with a ballerina, he can support, stabilize, lift, and turn her, allowing the partner to perform feats she could never do alone."[3]

What if we considered that our job as husbands and wives was "to make the beautiful more beautiful"? By supporting, stabilizing, lifting, and turning our spouses to the "best sides" of their strengths and personalities, our spouses can become more and do more than they ever could on their own. We essentially affirm the beauty we see in them by helping them become even more beautiful.

Some of our spouses may not even realize they *have* a best side. It's our job—and joy—to help them discover it. Others may have never allowed their best side to flourish—or even be seen—because they're insecure. If that's the case, when we learn to cherish them, we will provide the support they need.

"Showcasing"—making the deliberate mental shift to cherish our spouses by highlighting their beauty to others in the same way a dancer focuses on supporting his partner—is an essential part of learning how to cherish our spouses. If two dancers are each trying their hardest to be noticed above or even by each other, the performance is going to be a colossal, ugly failure.

Husbands can take the attitude of male dancers, seeking to showcase their wives' beauty. It may be the beauty of wisdom, so in social settings we do our best to ensure she is heard. It may be the beauty of leadership, and we support her so she can cast vision with others. It may be the beauty of hospitality, and we buy the things she needs and open up our homes (when we might prefer to be left alone) so her beauty can be on full display. We remind ourselves, "Today my job is to cherish her."

Very few marriages would ever approach divorce if each spouse would make one of their first daily comments to each other be this: "How can I support you today? How can I make your day better?"

If wives adopted this attitude, supporting their partners to perform feats they could never do on their own, they might soon be married to "different" husbands with the same names—more confident, more at peace, more engaged at home. What if a husband knew—in the deepest part of his soul—that his wife was his strongest support, his most encouraging partner? What would that do to him? What if he was willing to risk failure out in the world or at home with his kids because he knew in his wife's eyes he would always be her cherished champion? She supports him and stabilizes him, and when he fails, she binds up his wounds—spiritual and emotional—constantly turning and lifting him so his strongest side is always showing. What if every wife woke up and thought to herself, *Today my job is to cherish him by showcasing his best side to others?*

A Brilliant Match

Dr. Hugh Ross, a Canadian-American astrophysicist, captivated the attention of five thousand people at Second Baptist Church, Houston, as he made it seem patently ridiculous from scientific evidence alone to *not* believe in God. The ease with which he drew complicated numerical equations out of his mind—in response to spontaneous questions, not from prepared notes—left most of us feeling like we were thinking with a different species of brain. Yet, near the end of his talk, Dr. Ross confessed that he is "definitely on the autistic spectrum" and that if it wasn't for his wife, Kathy, he'd be in a much different place.

While a continuous line of autograph seekers waited to get Dr. Ross's autograph, Kathy told me her story of meeting a brilliant young Cal Tech researcher who was doing his postdoctoral studies while volunteering at a church.

Hugh was—and is—passionate about science and God; his intellect opened many doors that otherwise might have stayed shut, but his autistic tendencies were impairing his influence. As a friend, Kathy looked for ways to help him.

"What do I need to do?" Hugh asked her.

"Let's start with the haircut. And then the clothes. Stripes don't go with plaid, for instance. And you need pants that cover your socks, not to mention socks that match your pants. Try to use personal examples after you explain a spiritual/scientific principle so people can relate to what you're saying. Oh, and Hugh, this is very important: look at people when you talk to them; it makes a huge difference."

Kathy used a little more tact and grace than I've made it sound in this truncated form, but she remembers that Hugh literally took out a 3 x 5 card and jotted down notes as she talked. "Haircut. Clothes. Examples. Look people in the eye. Got it."

Hugh went to Macy's and asked the salesman to help him match clothes. He got a haircut, simply telling the hairdresser to make it look "normal." He concentrated not just on what he was saying but also on how he was saying it—including looking people in the eye.

The level of his impact took giant steps forward, which made Hugh all the more grateful to Kathy.

Kathy began to feel her heart moving romantically toward Hugh, but she told me she couldn't imagine that a man of Hugh's intellect and impact would be interested in her. Besides, with all the autistic stuff, how would that work out? Her heart was set first and foremost on serving God. "Heavenly Father," she had often prayed, "if I can help anyone come to know you, that's what I want to do."

That's why Kathy was so drawn to Hugh; she saw what Hugh was already doing on behalf of God's work on earth; but even more, she saw untapped potential if Hugh had just the right support. Perhaps she could reach more people helping Hugh than by sticking with her own ministry activities.

Hugh found his own heart yearning as well. In a matter-of-fact way typical of those on the autistic scale, his "romantic" invitation was as follows: "Kathy, I'd like to spend more time with you. With my studies and my work with the church, I have only one day off a week, but would you like to spend that one day off getting to know each other better?"

Believe it or not, that was enough to melt Kathy's heart. They dated, got engaged, and have been married for decades, faithfully serving God together.

I described the "marriage is ballet" metaphor to Kathy, and her eyes lit up; it describes her life. She found a brilliant but socially awkward man. By supporting, coaching, encouraging, and loving him, she has showcased his brilliance to the world. Many have come to embrace the gospel because of Hugh's witness and intellectual persuasion; others have had their faith solidified. And Kathy has been right beside Hugh the entire way.*

What makes the Rosses' marriage work so well is that Hugh doesn't fault Kathy for not being an astrophysicist, and Kathy doesn't expect Hugh to act like a man who doesn't have some lingering effects of autism. Hugh knows he wouldn't be where he is without Kathy, and Kathy believes her life's impact has been hugely enhanced by Hugh's ministry, not diminished. She's not

---

* If you want a picture of their impact, go to the website www.reasons.org.

embarrassed by his autism—she's proud of how God is using him. She has devoted her life to showcasing him.

In short, this is a couple that cherishes each other and that builds each other up. Because they accepted what each other was and wasn't, they actually became more than they would have been as individuals. They support, lift, turn, and showcase each other, allowing their partner to shine at what he or she does best.

Rather than having their love diminished by each other's imperfections, Kathy and Hugh cherish each other's gifts, showcase those gifts, and thus enhance those gifts. Together, they marvel at what God has done; the two of them have become far more as a team than either one ever would have been as an individual.

The beautiful has become yet more beautiful.

This is the power of cherish.

Making Music

When Leonard Bernstein, the famous orchestra conductor, was asked about the most difficult instrument to play, he surprised many by saying it was the *second* violin. "I can get plenty of first violinists, but to find one who plays second violin with as much enthusiasm, or second French horn, or second flute, that's a problem. And yet if no one plays second, we have no harmony."[4]

Learning to cherish means learning to be content playing second violin. This is at its root a very biblical thing to do. Jesus alluded to this when he said, "The Son of Man did not come to be served, but to serve" (Matthew 20:28). If we want to be like Jesus, we have to look for opportunities to play second violin. And though Jesus isn't explicitly addressing marriage in the above passage, marriage is certainly an ideal place to cultivate this attitude.

Beautiful, harmonic marriages are like the ballet and the symphony. They're not just one dancer or one note. They are built by asking ourselves on a regular basis, "Am I trying to showcase my spouse, or am I fixated on how my spouse is not showcasing me?"

The day you start thinking business success, ministry success, or personal happiness is more important to you than cherishing and showcasing your spouse is the day you stop cherishing your spouse and start feeling more distant from your spouse. *You're essentially having a love affair with yourself*, and you can't grow more intimate with your spouse when you're cherishing someone else.

It's spiritually impossible.

I want to make this clear: the more you focus on yourself, and have a love affair with yourself, the less you will cherish your spouse.

Imagine how silly it would seem if a newly engaged woman stuck out her left hand and said, "Don't pay any attention to the ring; notice my knuckle!" That's just how spiritually absurd it looks when in marriage we refuse to play "second violin" and put ourselves and our success over our love for our spouses.

A Different Kind of Pleasure

Learning to showcase our spouses in this way requires that we learn to appreciate a different kind of pleasure: our spouses' above our own.

Showcasing is the exact opposite of being selfish.

Worldly love loves because of what we get out of it:

"I love you because you make me feel so good."

"I love you because you make me happy."

"I love you because you are so lovable."

Infatuated couples don't *think* like this, but they do *feel* like this, which is why they can become so bitter and resentful when the infatuation fades and they have to try to rebuild an intimate marriage based on authenticity and service.

Be very careful if you've read Hugh and Kathy's story and your first thought was, *Yeah, why doesn't my spouse showcase me the way Kathy showcased Hugh?*

Cherishing our spouses isn't served by resenting our spouses but by showcasing them, which requires a certain self-forgetfulness and a corresponding determination to focus on our spouses. Another way to put it is that the call to cherish isn't to appreciate being pleasured by your spouse but to take pleasure in the pleasure of your spouse. To cherish is to be filled with joy not because your spouse brings you joy but because you take joy in your spouse's joy. You feel more elated over their blessings than even your own. To cherish is to almost desperately want others to see the best side of your spouse the way you do.

Picture a male dancer who has just supported, tossed, caught, turned, and showcased the ballerina, lifting her up for her final move—one that is so powerful and graceful and brilliant that when she lands in the spotlight, the audience leaps to their feet in a thunderous standing ovation.

And the male dancer slowly steps back into the shadows, his heart racing with exertion and pleasure.

The ballerina is adored, so his job is done. The standing ovation for her brings him great joy.

That's what it means to cherish.

Here's a curious truth some of you may find difficult to believe: the more you cherish your spouse, the more joy you'll have in your relationship. When you see others adore and admire your spouse, it makes your heart adore and admire your spouse that much more. Showcasing may seem like a strange backdoor to happiness, but I'm telling you, it works. When you get your highest joy by giving your spouse joy, *marriage takes off*.

When my friends Dennis and Barbara Rainey had a private marriage retreat shortly after they became empty nesters, they planned to spend time discussing what this season of life meant for Barbara and what it meant for Dennis. They never got to Dennis but instead spent three days planning out the implications for Barbara's new ministry opportunities.

Dennis is a busy man, the "top shepherd" in an organization with a budget in the tens of millions. But this man showed his integrity by agreeing to focus all their time on what his wife could do, discussing the support she would need in a new season of life. Dennis doesn't just talk about marriage and family; he lives it.

How can you better cherish your spouse so he or she can become the person God made them to be? What do you have to do in private? What do you have to do in public? What's the best way for you to showcase your particular spouse with their particular personality and gifts while helping them overcome their vulnerabilities and weaknesses?

If your spouse is an introvert, rather than push them onto center stage, it may mean making sure you stay by him or her in social situations because they need your support. You don't resent this—not if you cherish your spouse. You find comfort in knowing your spouse feels comfortable.

If your spouse needs time alone, showcasing may mean offering them opportunities to go off by themselves. You don't resent this or take it personally; instead, you find a quiet contentment knowing their needs are being met.

Showcasing is all about making the beautiful yet more beautiful.

In his book *Marriage Rebranded*, Tyler Ward writes, "If your spouse is not loved well, he or she may not live out their potential for good in the world . . . As we learn to love and therefore give to our spouse, we not only become the best version of ourselves—we offer our spouse the chance to become the best version of him or herself as well. Love, then, is giving for the sake of our spouse's becoming."[5]

Love is giving for the sake of our spouse's becoming.

Probably 90 percent of the couples who ask for my counsel have, at its root, the problem that both of them want to play first violin. The concept of cherishing—valuing someone, holding someone dear, wanting to showcase their beauty the way a new fiancée shows off her engagement ring, taking pleasure in your spouse's pleasure—helps us recapture a better, more productive, and more intimacy-enhancing mind-set.

You can have everything else right in marriage—you can even be perfectly compatible—but if you stop showcasing each other, the marriage will eventually grow stale, if not downright miserable. It doesn't matter how strong a dancer you are, men; you could have the arms of an Olympic champion and quadriceps like tree trunks, but if you drop your ballerina instead of catch her; if you step in front of her instead of lift her; if you flex your muscles instead of showcasing hers, that's going to be one ugly ballet performance.

Romance is fickle, unpredictable, and fragile. It comes and goes, usually without warning, sending both partners on a furious chase to recapture the spark. Cherishing expressed by showcasing is deliberate and intentional, and it provides a consistent path to ever-increasing marital intimacy and happiness.

CHERISHING CHERISH

- Christian marriage is like "relational ballet." By supporting, stabilizing, lifting, and turning our spouses to the "best sides" of their strength and personality, our spouses can become more and do more than they ever could on their own.

- A cherishing marriage is about learning to be content playing the second violin and making the beautiful yet more beautiful. We can't cherish our spouses if we're having a love affair with ourselves.

- The call to cherish isn't to appreciate being pleasured by your spouse but to take pleasure in the pleasure of your spouse.

- Showcasing means highlighting a partner's strengths in public—making the beautiful yet more beautiful—and nurturing them in private.

- The more you cherish someone, the more joy you get out of your marriage. When you get your highest joy by giving your spouse joy, *marriage takes off.*

QUESTIONS FOR
DISCUSSION AND REFLECTION

1. Discuss the trust that must exist between ballet partners—the woman trusting the man to catch her, the man learning to turn her to the crowd and knowing she must trust him. How can that image impact the way you look at marriage?

2. Gary says that sometimes our spouses may not even realize they have a "best side." What strengths or gifts might your spouse be unaware of that you can cultivate and bring out of him or her?

3. How does having a "love affair with yourself" make it impossible to fully enjoy marriage with your spouse?

4. Hugh and Kathy Ross are both realistic about each other's strengths and shortcomings. Cherishing each other doesn't call us to deny reality, but rather to accept and perhaps even improve reality (which we'll discuss in later chapters). Describe what cherishing each other, at its highest ideal, would look like in your marriage. Be specific and personal.

5. How can you best "showcase your spouse's beauty" in the coming month? Think of at least one or two concrete examples.

6. After reading this chapter, what do you think is the difference between cherishing your spouse and being infatuated with your spouse?

CHAPTER 4

Your Honor

Cherishing means noticing and honoring each other

A husband and wife sat in front of me at church—the husband was also seated next to a male friend. Every time the pastor said something that was funny or insightful, the husband looked toward his friend and shared the moment. At the exact same time, the wife looked to her husband with a palpable expectation in her eyes that melted when she saw he was turned the other way.

This went on three or four times.

By the fifth time, she stopped looking.

She stared straight ahead with a fixed expression on her face that could have frozen the planet Mercury.

Still, the husband didn't notice. He was having a fantastic time sharing moments of insight and laughter with his friend.

I've talked to enough couples that I could easily imagine the conversation on the way home.

"What's wrong, honey?"

"Nothing."

"You seem angry."

"Why would I be?"

"I don't have a clue. That's why I asked you."

This answer, of course, makes her even angrier. Which makes him angry in turn and think she's being even more unreasonable.

Here's why she's angry: She doesn't feel cherished. She wants to share life with you, and you're (perhaps unintentionally) sharing it with a buddy instead. It sounds so innocuous to you: "I'm just sharing a moment with my friend; am I not supposed to have any other friends?" But you know she wants you to have other friends.

She also wants to be cherished. You ended up ignoring your wife, treating her as if she wasn't even there. Making a spouse feel invisible is the opposite of cherish and creates feelings of alienation instead of belonging.

The issue isn't your friend any more than the issue isn't ultimately a hobby, a job, a video game, a child, or even an addiction.

The issue is *honor.* The issue is *being noticed.*

If we want to cherish our spouses, we have to keep noticing them, which is another way of saying we have to keep honoring them.

Passive Hurt

If you asked most men to define emotional abuse, 90 percent of us would say, "Yelling, shouting, screaming out cruel things, using hurtful words."

And we'd be half right.

Emotional abuse is also the *withholding* of love, encouragement, and support. It can be a sin of deprivation every bit as much as a sin of commission. Look at it this way: if a man responds to hurt with the silent treatment, he could say he's not doing anything wrong because he's not saying anything mean, but in that context the silence itself is hurtful (deliberately so, in most cases). That's emotional abuse.

Since the vast majority of us promise on our wedding day to "love and cherish" each other till "death do us part," a man or woman's desire to be cherished by their spouse is reasonable, so withholding cherish can rise to the level of emotional abuse. It is a reasonable (not "needy") desire to be noticed and honored by our spouses, just as it is a reasonable desire for a young child to be fed by her parents.

Every time a wife or husband looks at their spouse to share a moment and sees their lover preoccupied with someone or something else, it feels like they've taken a relational ice bucket over the head.

It kills intimacy.

University of Washington professor and marriage expert Dr. John Gottman writes, "Without honor, all the marriage skills one can learn won't work."[6]

Honoring our spouses is an essential part of what it means to cherish. To honor someone is to hold them in high esteem. When a queen greets you, you bow or curtsy. When a judge enters the courtroom, you stand. When a cherished spouse enters the room or says something, you honor and cherish them by taking notice.

You can honor someone without cherishing them, but you can't cherish someone without honoring them. When you fail to cherish a spouse, you are essentially dishonoring them.

Dr. Gottman insists that without honor, we won't have

happy marriages. We won't have intimate marriages. We won't have successful marriages. If we try to apply brilliant marital "tips" (communication exercises, love languages, conflict resolution) but leave out a focus on honoring and cherishing each other, it's like lighting a candle and then depriving it of oxygen. The flame will have a very short life. No strategy will work without being fed by the fresh air of cherishing.

The Invisible Woman

Men, look at the music women create, and you'll get a picture of how so many feel dishonored by men. Aretha Franklin stormed to the top of the charts with her famous song in the seventies that demanded a little "R-E-S-P-E-C-T." More recently, an all-female group with the fortuitous (for our purposes) name Cherish released a single titled "Unappreciated." At the beginning of 2016, the video had already passed *seven and a half million* views. Cherish apparently speaks for millions of women when they sing, "And lately I've been feeling unappreciated/When you're here, it's like I'm invisible."

I hear that last sentiment a lot: "It's like I'm invisible." Nicole Johnson wrote an entire book on "the invisible woman," describing how so many wives feel invisible in their own homes.[7] They speak, and no one listens. No one asks their opinion, just occasionally their permission. These wives might go to a dinner party with their husbands, watch their men look into another woman's eyes, seem interested, and ask her questions to draw out the conversation—and it hurts like crazy that she can't remember the last time her husband looked at her like that or asked her a question like that or listened to her like that. And as soon as they get in the car to go home, her invisibility swallows her up. She now knows her husband is still capable of cherishing a woman—she's seen it in action!—so why can't he cherish *her*? The next day she walks into a living room filled with her husband and children, says something, and nobody even responds, as if she doesn't even exist.

She's invisible.

In her own home.

Not doing something right *is* doing something wrong.

One husband I know gives his children a split second to look up whenever their mom starts talking to them. If the kids don't respond *immediately*, he turns off whatever they're looking at.

"Are you intentionally ignoring your mother right now?" he'll ask. "Because that's not gonna fly in this house. If you can't pull yourself away from whatever you're watching, I'll do it for you without pausing it or saving it. Whenever your mom speaks, she gets your attention."

His wife never feels invisible; she feels cherished.

It's about Honor

During the time I wrote this book, I'd ask wives what makes them feel cherished, and it was like releasing a pack of hounds after an English fox—they were off and running with their answers. When I'd ask husbands, "How do you feel cherished by your wife?" I'd get quizzical looks—"What are you talking about?"

Many men think cherish is something wives want, and they feel like less of a man even using that word. So I learned to ask my question in a different way: "What does your wife do that makes you feel special? Honored? Noticed?"

And the most typical response was, "Well, do you want the PG answer or the real answer?"

I know this will sound like a cliché, but for a large percentage of men, if they're not noticed between the sheets, everything that happens outside the bedroom is negated. I'd say this is particularly true when a husband is in his twenties, thirties, and forties. A wife usually can't overestimate the vulnerability a man in that season of life feels toward sex. As a pastor, I often encounter younger husbands, and I'm reminded of the near-daily assault many men feel trying to live lives of integrity in a pornographic world.

Women, it may help to think of your husband's sexual desires as a request to be honored. Many men work so hard, not just to contribute to the family budget, but to be true to their marital vows. There are plenty of spiritual and physical forces trying to inject compromise into your man's soul. Your physical affection is a way of honoring his commitment, his battle, and his physical desires.

The husbands I talked to who felt most cherished by their wives—most *honored*—felt spoiled in the sexual department. They want a wife who proclaims, "He is altogether desirable. This is my beloved and this is my friend" (Song of Songs 5:16 ESV).

In the same way that a woman wants to be noticed and taken seriously when she speaks, enters a room, calls her husband, and doesn't want him looking at his smartphone while he's supposed to be talking to her, so husbands want to be noticed in the dark.

Your husband probably doesn't use this language, but he feels dishonored when you want to do a hundred different tasks besides making love. When your husband is younger and feels like he's taking second place to the children and when the frequency of sexual intimacy is placed far behind laundry and only slightly ahead of cleaning out the gutters, it's like when you're talking to your husband and you suddenly realize he hasn't heard a single word of what you have been saying.

Dishonored.

A key principle to honoring your spouse is understanding that the person being honored gets to determine how they want to be honored. That's just the way it works, spiritually and psychologically. During one particularly hot Boston marathon, I ran by a family handing out frozen ice pops. The pops were pure sugar and water, and being frozen, they were very cold, and I will feel grateful to that thoughtful family for the rest of my life. It was a perfect treat in the second half of a hot marathon.

Every other marathon I've run has legions of people handing out Vaseline. Chafing can be an issue, but I've learned to prepare for that problem ahead of time, so I've never—not once in thirteen marathons—stopped and taken the offered Vaseline.

But every race has people offering me some.

Your husband won't feel noticed if you're trying to hand him Vaseline when what he really wants is a frozen pop. His needs will determine what makes him feel honored, and if Vaseline isn't a need, he can't be all that grateful when you offer it. If what he really wants is a wife who puts more time and thought into sex, and yet she tries to do everything else, he won't feel honored or cherished.

He'll feel *invisible*.

I know you hate feeling that way, so perhaps this image will help you understand what it feels like for a husband who feels ignored in the bedroom.

Of course, it goes both ways. An increasing number of wives are hurting because their husband's libido is lower than theirs. They want to be cherished as Solomon cherished his love in Song of Songs: "How fair and pleasant you are, O loved one, delectable maiden" (7:6 NRSV), so that the wife brags, "I am my beloved's, and his desire is for me" (7:10 NRSV).

Men, when your wives hear other wives talk about their husbands' constant sexual pursuit and your wife can't even remember the last time you approached her, she feels dishonored as well. This is no longer a men-always-want-it and women-can-take-it-or-leave-it world—it never really was. Some men lose interest because of health issues, especially weight gain and diet. Other men mess up their brains by looking at porn. Whatever the cause (I'm not talking about physical inability due to age or disease), sexually neglected or sexually unpursued women rarely feel cherished.

Men, our sexual expression isn't about getting our needs met but about honoring our wives by affirming their beauty, their loveliness, and their desirability. They feel noticed when they are wanted. In an age of pornography, we have to "conserve" our sexual interest and save it for our marriages so our wives feel duly desired and cherished. Sexual longing is a part of cherishing and honoring each other: "Marriage should be honored by all, and the marriage bed kept pure" (Hebrews 13:4).

Outdo One Another

Romans 12:10 tells us to "outdo one another in showing honor" (NRSV). While not specifically addressing marriage, if this is true of members within the church, it should be *especially* true between a husband and wife. We are literally commanded to "outdo" our spouses in showing honor to them. Here's a colloquial way of saying this:

> "Try every day to cherish your wife more than she cherishes you."
> "Try every day to cherish your husband more than he cherishes you."

Don't we naturally do the opposite? Instead of asking how we can cherish our spouses, we obsess over, "Why can't they love me the way I love them?"

Your biblical call is to focus on outdoing your spouse in showing honor. Your best efforts should be to honor him even more than he honors you. You might even think, *I'm kind of glad he sets the bar a little lower; otherwise, I couldn't be faithful to the command to outdo him.*

How do you think your marriage would change if both of you (or even one of you) woke up with a goal every day to outdo your spouse in showing her or him honor? You'd have to plan. You'd have to set a few things in motion. And that's the motivation behind cherish: an active pursuit of honoring, showcasing, paying attention, serving, adoring.

At the end of the day, instead of being resentful that you seemed to give more love than you received, there will be a joy that you are walking in obedience. You aimed to outdo your spouse in showing honor, and you succeeded. You won't point this out to your spouse, of course, or you'd undercut the entire day's efforts. Instead, you'll take quiet comfort in the fact that you are doing God's will.

One practical way to learn to outdo your spouse in showing honor is to try to "catch more bids" than your spouse catches.

Catching Bids

Dr. John Gottman assigned couples into two groups—the "masters" and "disasters"—when he researched what was directly related to a couple's happiness. He notes that throughout each person's day, one partner will make regular "bids" for the other's attention. In our language, we could describe these bids as the question, "Do you still cherish me?"

What the spouse does in response to these bids has a huge impact on marital connection and happiness.

Writing for *The Atlantic*, Emily Esfahani Smith explains:

> Throughout the day, partners would make requests for connections, what Gottman calls "bids." For example, say that the husband is a bird enthusiast and notices a goldfinch fly across the yard. He might say to his wife, "Look at that beautiful bird outside!" He's not just commenting on the bird here: he's requesting a response from his wife—a sign of interest or support—hoping they'll connect, however momentarily, over the bird.
>
> The wife now has a choice. She can respond by either "turning toward" or "turning away" from her husband, as Gottman puts it. Though the bird-bid might seem minor and silly, it can actually reveal a lot about the health of the relationship. The husband thought the bird was important enough to bring it up in conversation and the question is whether his wife recognizes and respects that.
>
> People who turned toward their partners in the study responded by engaging the bidder, showing interest and support in the bid. Those who didn't—those who turned away—would not respond or respond minimally and

continue doing whatever they were doing, like watching TV or reading the paper. Sometimes they would respond with overt hostility, saying something like, "Stop interrupting me, I'm reading."

These bidding interactions had profound effects on marital well-being. Couples who had divorced after a six-year follow up had "turn-toward bids" 33 percent of the time. Only three in ten of their bids for emotional connection were met with intimacy. The couples who were still together after six years had "turn-toward bids" 87 percent of the time. Nine times out of ten, they were meeting their partner's emotional needs.[8]

Dr. Gottman's work demonstrates that if we want to cherish our spouses, we must learn to take an active interest in what interests them. That's what it means to honor and notice. We can practice listening and then responding, aiming to get our "turn-toward bids" up to at least 90 percent. This is helpful for me, as it teaches me that whenever my wife expresses an opinion, reads something interesting from the local paper, or makes an observation, I am either cherishing her or neglecting her. There is no middle ground here. Her bid is either met or rejected. Cherishing is expressed, or it's not. Intimacy is built, or it is assaulted, even in the most mundane marital conversations.

Think of a baseball hitter at the plate. Once the pitch is thrown, it counts. The batter can let the ball go by, swing and miss, or hit the ball. But the pitch counts. Every time your spouse makes a "bid," a pitch is thrown and you have a decision to make. *Not* to make a decision is actually a decision—in this case, a destructive and hurtful one.

Look at it this way: whenever your spouse seeks your attention—of any kind and in any room in the house—what he or she is essentially asking is, "Do you still cherish me?"

Good News

If you believe you have been dishonoring your spouse by not noticing him or her, the good news is that Dr. Gottman insists that honoring can be learned and practiced and improved on. As just one example, he and his wife, Julie, also a psychologist, discovered that the way a spouse treats good news on behalf of the other spouse pays huge dividends. If a wife finally gets a book contract and the husband makes a big deal about it, sharing in her joy, celebrating with her, and cheering her on, that goes a long way toward making her feel honored. If he underplays it: "That's all you got for the advance? Are you sure they're not taking advantage of you?" the damage done to the marriage is significant. She feels *dishonored*.

Here's how we might summarize noticing and honoring: *sharing the lows with empathy and celebrating the highs with enthusiasm.*

If you're cherishing your spouse, you'll ask questions: "That's fantastic! When is the book due? Do you know who your editor will be? How long do you have to finish it? What do I need to do to give you more time to write and revise?" Those kinds of questions show genuine interest and support and make the partner feel like you truly care.

Think of cherishing this way: If *you* had been the one to get that contract, those are the questions you would be asking on your own behalf. By asking them of your spouse, you're entering into their celebration. You're noticing them. You're honoring them. And so they feel cherished.

The size or scope of your spouse's accomplishment doesn't matter. Whether it's a woman getting tenure or finally getting a closet cleaned out, she just wants what she does to be validated. I can't say this too often: Whatever she does, husband, validate. Whatever he does, wife, validate. Value it. Cherish it. Support him. Encourage her. Value it as much as you would if you were the one doing it.

Dishonored

Noticing and honoring are both like paddling against the natural drift toward dishonoring in the sense that if we don't keep paddling (honoring and noticing), we'll be carried in the opposite direction. The work is never done.

Early on in their marriage, Kevin called Alyssa several times a day. Alyssa felt comforted because it meant she always knew where Kevin was. When the kids were young and Alyssa was staying home, she'd frequently get *two* calls before lunch.

"It made me feel so good," Alyssa remembers, "just having him ask about me and the kids."

What she's saying is she felt noticed—which made her feel honored—and that made her feel cherished.

When cell phones came out, Kevin often texted Alyssa with "sweet nothings." It was amazing how one sentence with no capitalization or punctuation could still make Alyssa feel honored, simply because it signified that Kevin was thinking about her.

About ten years into the marriage, something changed. At first, there'd be just one call before lunch, then one call all day, and then only an occasional text. The lack of noticing signaled a change in Kevin's heart.

Kevin traveled quite a bit for his job, and for the first decade he never went to sleep in a hotel without first calling Alyssa to say good night. But now, Alyssa could go for days without hearing from him while he was gone.

Days.

At first, Alyssa tried not to think about it. Inside, it made her feel "he doesn't even care what the kids and I are doing today," but the implications of that line of thought were so frightful that she didn't want to dwell on it.

When Kevin came home, Alyssa felt like she had to overcompensate: "I was so used to telling him about my day—usually in small increments—that now I felt like I had to get it all out in one long conversation. He didn't want to hear it, but I thought as long as I could tell him about my day, it would somehow keep us connected. Instead, it just overwhelmed him."

Alyssa wanted to be noticed, but Kevin didn't want to notice her. Alyssa thought if she could just force Kevin to notice her, maybe the marriage could be saved, but it doesn't work that way.

Then came a fateful New Year's Eve. Kevin was working in Washington, D.C., and called Alyssa at 10:00 p.m. to check in. Alyssa called him back at midnight to celebrate the moment together, but Kevin didn't answer his phone.

"If Kevin wasn't wearing his phone, he was never separated from it by more than six inches, and he *never* turned it off. When his voice mail message came on, it felt like a punch in the gut."

The next day, Alyssa asked Kevin about it, and he said, "Huh. I guess I just didn't hear it."

That's when Alyssa knew her worst fears were being realized. Kevin's "assistant" was no longer just an assistant, and

Kevin even admitted she had been with him in Washington, D.C. Alyssa raised the issue about this assistant over the course of several weeks, and Kevin eventually promised he'd get her reassigned, but in reality, he was planning to take her with him on a business trip to Hawaii.

When Alyssa found out, everything came together in three frightful words: "I've been replaced."

She felt dishonored.

Invisible.

Instead of feeling like a cherished wife, she felt like a bothersome nuisance.

Husbands, our wives should never in a million lifetimes feel like they are a *nuisance* to us. That is the exact opposite of cherish. They need to see our eyes light up and our arms spread wide whenever they send a bid our way.

Kevin tried to defend his decision not to reassign his assistant by saying, "I have to think about her well-being," but all Alyssa could think was, "What about *my* well-being? What about your kids?"

Any objective person could see Alyssa's point, but the reason Kevin was blinded to it was that he had begun cherishing someone else. When you cherish someone, you put that person's needs above everyone else's—that's what it means to cherish. And Kevin's lack of noticing and honoring Alyssa signified that he now cherished someone above her.

You can sadly guess the ending. It isn't a story with a happy ending. Kevin and his assistant moved in together, and though he still occasionally makes bids for Alyssa to take him back, he won't let go of his relationship with his assistant until Alyssa agrees to return. This doesn't make Alyssa feel like she's Eve, the only woman in the world. It makes her feel like Kevin is getting a little tired of his assistant and now views Alyssa as perhaps his best available option—for the moment.

The act of consistently noticing and honoring our spouses cultivates and maintains a certain kind of relationship, *and it shapes our hearts*. Noticing and honoring sustain the force and power of cherishing. When we stop noticing and stop honoring our spouses in the little things, the relationship starves. Husbands and wives want more than mere commitment; they want attention; they want interest and want to be noticed; they want to matter. They want their bids to be "caught."

They want to be honored.

Alyssa urges husbands, "Always be interested in what your wife is saying, even if you don't want to hear the details. Sometimes Kevin would tell me, 'Hey, I know you like to give me all the details, but how about the *Reader's Digest* version?' But that made me feel like I was just bothering him, like he was listening to me out of duty, not desire. I certainly didn't feel cherished.

"If you want your wife to feel cherished, call her at work or home during the day, even if it's just for twenty seconds. That at least tells her you're thinking about her. You've noticed her, even while you're away from each other."

The last thing a cherished husband or wife should feel is *invisible*. A cherished spouse feels noticed. A cherished spouse feels pursued. A cherished spouse feels honored.

If frequent calls are something you *used* to do and if sex is something you *used* to have, just know you've slipped away from cherishing. That slide can take you to the worst of places, even divorce.

Noticing each other, honoring each other, and connecting with each other do take time. But don't you enjoy your marriage more when each of you cherishes the other?

My Boneheaded Mistake

After all we've learned from John and Julie Gottman about what we should do to notice and honor our spouses, allow me to offer an example of what *not* to do. After writing the first draft of this chapter (I was in a hotel room), I went in to wake up my wife, who promptly told me about her dream.

"Do you remember your dreams?" she asked me.

"Not usually."

"When you do, are they good or bad?"

"Usually bad, if I remember them."

"Yeah, well, I read that could be a vitamin B6 deficiency."

"What?"

"If you don't remember your dreams or they're always bad, it could mean you have a lack of vitamin B6."

I laughed. Readers of my blog and books know my wife is very into holistic medicine, organic, fair trade, gluten-free, pasture-raised, grass-fed, non-GMO, locally raised, no partially hydrogenated anything, no sugar, etc., but this was too much for me. So I laughed. In this case, what she was saying seemed absurd.

Then I realized what I had just done. She had shared something to be helpful. She shared something that mattered to her, and she was expecting a thoughtful response, not a cruel dismissal. Besides, she had read studies—I just had completely uninformed opinions.

And in my act of laughing, I completely dishonored her.

So I apologized. "I'm sorry, honey; you've read those studies. What do I know? I'm not a doctor. Thanks for sharing that."

Even better, I should have asked her how I could increase my vitamin B6 intake.

The idea that vitamin B6 could influence dreams stills seems questionable to me, but this conversation wasn't really about the power of B6 to affect dreams; it was about whether my wife would wake up feeling cherished or disrespected. Unfortunately, I chose disrespect—even after studying the article about "turn-toward bids" and writing about it.

Which means, if I aim to hit 90 percent in this round, I need to catch the next nine bids.

This is a journey, friends—not something we will master overnight.

CHERISHING CHERISH

- The call to cherish is an active call to notice and honor our spouses, so passive neglect in marriage (whether intentional or not) can be considered a form of emotional abuse.

- When wives aren't honored, they feel invisible.

- Attention inside and outside the bedroom is often a matter of *honor*.

- Scripture calls us to outdo our spouses in showing them honor.

- Studies have shown that our spouses will regularly throw out "bids" for our attention; we should look at these bids as questions: "Do you still cherish me?"

- In the happiest of marriages, the "masters" have a turn-toward bid rate of nearly 90 percent. We can learn to pay attention to these bids; it's an improvable skill.

- For our spouses to feel cherished, it is particularly important that we respond to their good news with excitement and interest and draw out more information with questions.

- The simple act of staying connected via phone calls or texts is essential to each spouse's feeling of being cherished.

QUESTIONS FOR DISCUSSION AND REFLECTION

1. Describe a time or season when you felt a little neglected by your spouse. What happened? How did it make you feel?

2. Describe a season when you now realize you may have neglected your spouse or made them a lesser priority. What did you do? Why did you do it—were you too busy or distracted? Was it unintentional?

3. What is a healthy way for a spouse who feels invisible to make the situation known?

4. Do you agree that not cherishing your spouse may be seen as a form of emotional abuse? Why or why not?

5. How does the call to view fulfilling your spouse's sexual desires as honoring them change the way a couple can view sexual intimacy?

6. What would you have to do differently if you committed to outdoing your spouse in showing honor over the next seven days?

7. Think back over the past week. Try to remember three turn-toward bids that your spouse threw your way. How did you respond? If you can't remember any, ask your spouse to remind you.

8. Since we're aiming at a 90 percent response, evaluate your current turn-toward bid rate. Are you already at 90 percent? 70 percent? Less than 50 percent? In a spirit of humility, ask your spouse what he or she thinks.

9. When is the last time your spouse received some really good news? How would you grade your engagement and response (on a scale from A to F)?

CHAPTER 5

When Cherishing Goes to War

Cherishing is about protecting
each other and killing contempt

He's not a chef; he's a cook!"

"He can call me a chef—"

"No, he can't, because you're not. A chef makes things from scratch. You just heat things up. It's not the same thing."

I had been trying to involve a quiet man in the discussion, so I brought up what he did, referring to him as a chef: "Don't chefs usually like such and such . . ."

His wife jumped on the offensive, declaring that her husband was *not* a chef, and no one in the entire universe should *ever* use that label when referring to her husband.

Her husband works at a retirement home, preparing meals for two hundred residents. The budget is tight, and time is even tighter. Administrators have a tendency to see what the minimum requirement is, cost-wise, and then ask the head guy (this husband) to get by on 10 percent less. So, yes (sadly), a lot of the meals are frozen and heated up. "I have to come up with three different entrees for every meal," the husband explained.

"The people there don't even care what the food tastes like anyway," the wife countered.

"Yes, they *do*," the husband responded with a quiet forcefulness. "They really do."

As an objective observer, I saw a man in a difficult situation—trying to feed two hundred senior citizens as best he could on a limited budget. And I saw a wife who was determined to denigrate this effort as so common and perhaps even somewhat shameful that she didn't want anyone to accidentally give her husband more respect than he was due.

Why can't she see the nobility of a man who is giving his all to try to bring daily pleasure and nutrition on a tight budget to two hundred senior citizens? That's a good thing, isn't it? He doesn't set the budget. He doesn't declare the limitations. He just tries to do his best in the midst of it.

Why wouldn't a wife want to pray for and with her husband that he would make a difference in senior citizens' lives? Why not ask God to work through her husband—as Jesus fed crowds with a few loaves and fish? Perhaps God could gift this man to bring some miracle of health and enjoyment on scarce provisions.

Cherishing calls us to go to war against contempt. That's because cherishing is all about protecting our spouses—their reputation, their personhood, their sense of value and worth.

The Cycle of Contempt

Look at a newly dating and infatuated couple—the men's and women's faces are lit up. You see them all the time at the airport.

The eye contact between the two is intense. They stand close; they gaze deeply at each other, almost as if they are afraid to blink. They can't get farther than eighteen inches apart without drifting back into direct contact thirty seconds later.

But from that pinnacle of cherishing often comes the sad cycle of contempt. Remember that cliché—"familiarity breeds contempt"? Nothing is more familiar than marriage. Marriage to a less than perfect person, absent an understanding of grace and a commitment to cherish, can lead to disappointment, which leads to frustration, which leads to bitterness, which leads to contempt.

Here's how it works spiritually:

Disappointment → Frustration → Bitterness → Contempt

This is a *spiritual* journey before it is a marital one, and contempt unleashes the "death spiral." It feeds itself and gets hungrier as it grows. Instead of gazing at each other as the couples at the airport do, couples with contempt stare like a dagger at the ground or off to the side when their spouse is talking—they can't bear to look at them except when they're ready to pounce back with a verbal assault. Then their eyes are locked and loaded, but to fire away, not to adore, not to understand. You've never seen impatience like you've seen it in the eyes of a spouse who is just waiting for her spouse to stop talking, to take one-tenth of a breath, so she can jump in and explain how he couldn't be more wrong, and she has proof.

It even leads to bizarre behavior. An angry wife literally screamed at her husband in my office, "See, you don't listen to me; you won't even answer my question!"—*after he had just gently and calmly answered her question.* Her contempt was so thick that she couldn't hear what he was saying, even though it was her critique of him. She was, at least at that moment, blinded and deafened by her contempt.

Dr. John Gottman believes contempt is the "greatest predictor of divorce."[9] He defines contempt as an attitude of superiority, evidenced by speaking down to your partner through name calling or direct insults. This is, of course, the exact opposite of how we have defined cherish, which opens our eyes to our spouses' excellence, which is why cherish is the best antidote to contempt.

Ironically, an attitude of superiority and speaking down to a partner is one of the most common failings of people who consider themselves mature Christians and who are married to "less mature" believers. Because they see themselves as "better"—they would never use that word, but the concept drives their thinking—in the Lord, they start to define their spouses by their sins and failings, and it becomes a snowball that leads to an attitude of superiority and hypernegativity. They don't realize their own attitude is the single biggest assault on their marriage, even more than what they're criticizing in their spouses. They think they are the mature ones for noticing the fault, not realizing they are the most destructive partners because they're obsessing over the fault.

Couples committed to cherishing each other do go to war, but never with each other. They go to war against contempt, always seeking to protect each other. This is how you know you're cherishing your spouse: *you're protecting him or her instead of attacking them.*

On a terrifying day in 1981, Ronald Reagan, the fortieth president of the United States, was leaving the Washington Hilton Hotel when a would-be assassin sent a "devastator bullet" (designed to explode on impact) into the president's left side.

The day after the assassination attempt, when the severity of the hit was fully understood, Nancy Reagan sought spiritual comfort from Donn Moomaw, their pastor in California. They were joined at a White House meeting by Frank Sinatra and his wife, as well as by Billy Graham. Nancy unburdened herself there, confessing to the small circle, "I'm really struggling with a feeling of failed responsibility. I usually stand at Ronnie's left side. And that's where he took the bullet."[10]

What Nancy was really saying was, *I wish it had hit me instead of him. If I had been with him, I'm the one who would be in the hospital.*

A wife who cherishes her husband wants to protect him; a husband who cherishes his wife wants to put himself in harm's way on her behalf. This is the positive side of cherish, which makes the negative—*contempt*—all but unthinkable. Cherishing our spouses shapes our minds and our hearts to such an extent that every cell in our body wants to protect, honor, and thank our cherished spouses, regardless of the cost to us.

We don't have to wait for an assassin's assault to "protect" our spouses, however. Protecting can be as common an act as our sparing them from an awkward social situation.

Taking the Hit

The first thing Carlos said when he walked into my office was, "I just want you to know I was here six minutes early. Rosa was late. I'm sorry."

Rosa looked at her husband and said, "Thanks for throwing me under the bus."

We had met several times before, so it was time to deal with this. "Carlos," I said, "five years from now, you might not even remember my name. Tonight, you'll go home with Rosa and I'll go home to my wife, and neither of us will think about the other. The reason you threw Rosa under the bus is that you're worried about what I'm thinking of you; you should be more concerned about what Rosa thinks of you. She's the one you're living with.

"If you had said, 'Look, Gary, I'm sorry we're late,' Rosa would have thought, *Wow, he protected me*, and you'd have an entirely different experience at home tonight. Your job is to honor and protect Rosa because that's who you're going home with. It's not to impress me. Focus on her."

Carlos had a chance to "take the hit" for Rosa, and in doing so, he could have made her feel protected. And in making her feel protected, she would have felt cherished.

In retrospect, the stakes were so small. I've seen a lot of couples, and I'd have to press myself to remember who "Carlos" actually is.* But I guarantee you his wife knows who he is. It is so much more important how his wife feels about him than how I do.

But then I had to speak to Rosa. Her tardiness had come up several times before, and it was really bugging Carlos. "Rosa, you know how you felt when Carlos threw you under the bus?"

"Yes!"

"That's how he feels every time you make him late to a meeting. He can't *not* feel that way. He respects being on time. He hates—literally hates—being late. So when you make him late, he's going to feel terrible. He can forgive you. He can learn to not throw you under the bus. But he can't stop caring about being late. He just can't. You honor and protect him by working hard to be somewhere on time."

---

* I just know his name wasn't really Carlos.

You see, in her own way, Rosa wasn't protecting Carlos either. Instead of caring what Carlos felt about being on time, she was more concerned with how she looked or getting a last-minute task done than with honoring her husband.

What I love about the call to cherish each other is that it's an active decision to ask ourselves on a regular basis, "What do I need to do to protect my spouse?" Asking this question pushes us toward acts of cherishing. For Carlos and Rosa, cherishing means protecting each other's reputation, but it has to be applied in completely different ways. In this case, neither one was cherishing the other.

A quick caveat: "protecting" your spouse doesn't mean enabling an addiction. An untreated addiction or covering up a pattern of abuse isn't protecting your spouse; it's enabling them to continue on a destructive path.

Forget Them!

Sometimes we have to be protected from ourselves. We can be our own worst enemies.

Donnie grew up as a people-pleasing Southern boy. Jaclyn, his wife, grew up in Pennsylvania with the "attitude of a Yankee." "I don't deal with people pleasing," Jaclyn says. "We don't worry about that kind of thing in Pennsylvania."

Because Jaclyn and Donnie work together, Jaclyn sees how much of a toll it takes on Donnie when a customer isn't pleased. It tears Donnie apart. He frets even when it's not his fault because he just can't stand it when others don't think well of him. But that can be a dangerous trait in the business world.

For instance, their on-site camera once recorded one of their employees stealing from them. At first, Donnie practically blamed himself: "We try so hard to treat our employees well. I want to be the best employer in the world. Why would he do that?"

Jaclyn has a rejoinder for these moments of self-doubt: "Forget him!" (She doesn't exactly say "forget" him, and while it's not a swearword, it's not the most family-friendly expression either, so we'll stick with "forget him.")

Another work relationship Donnie struggled with was pushed to the breaking point. Donnie went out of his way to please a person who just couldn't be pleased, so he felt like a failure. "Forget him!" Jaclyn shouted with all the passion of a concerned wife. "That's *his* character, not yours. This is about *him*, not you. Forget him!"

With this phrase, Jaclyn saves Donnie from himself. She protects him from the unreasonable demands and actions of the outside world. And she's helped him move forward in their business. Donnie knows he needs these reminders, and he cherishes Jaclyn for offering them.

In the letter to the Colossians, the apostle Paul wrote that he was "completing what is lacking in Christ's afflictions for the sake of his body, that is, the church" (Colossians 1:24 NRSV). Paul isn't suggesting Christ's suffering is insufficient—not at all. It's rather that Paul knows the church in Corinth is young and fragile, and in the words of N. T. Wright, "It is as if he, as the leader of the church in that part of the world, is drawing the enemy fire on to himself so that the young church may have a breathing space, a time to grow." Wright suggests Paul's attitude as he sits in prison in Ephesus (where Paul wrote the letter to the Colossians) is, "Well, as long as they are concentrating on me, then Christ's body, the church, can grow until it is strong enough to stand on its own feet."[11]

In a sense, Jaclyn takes Donnie's enemy fire onto herself. She lifts Donnie out of being perhaps a bit too concerned about others' opinions. His tendency to be a people pleaser doesn't make her cherish him less—she clearly delights in who he is, but at the same time, she wants to protect him from letting others define him. This cherishing attitude serves their marriage and is helping Donnie to become stronger and a little less dependent on the opinions of others.

Ask yourself, "Where is my spouse weak? Where is my spouse fragile? How in that situation can I draw the enemy fire onto myself until he or she is stronger and more mature?"

The Number One Threat

Dr. John Gottman and his wife, Julie, explain how contempt is cultivated, as opposed to an attitude we've been calling cherishing:

> "There's a habit of mind that the masters have," Gottman explained in an interview, "which is this: they are scanning the social environment for things they can appreciate and say thank you for. They are building this culture of respect and appreciation very purposefully. Disasters are scanning the social environment for partners' mistakes."
>
> "It's not just scanning environment," chimed in Julie Gottman. "It's scanning the *partner* for what the *partner* is doing right or scanning him for what he's doing wrong and criticizing versus respecting him and expressing appreciation."
>
> Contempt, they have found, is the number one factor that tears couples apart. People who are focused on criticizing their partners miss a whopping 50 percent of

positive things their partners are doing and they see negativity when it's not there. People who give their partner the cold shoulder—deliberately ignoring the partner or responding minimally—damage the relationship by making their partner feel worthless and invisible, as if they're not there, not valued . . . Being mean is the death knell of relationships.[12]

When you're talking to a couple mired in contempt, you feel like you're in a bipolar situation. I've heard a wife say, "He's such a good father," five minutes before she says, "He's completely alienated the children."

"He's a good man"—and then, "I can't live with him anymore."

By their own words, these wives recognize their husbands have many fine qualities, but they define them by the things that need to be worked on, even though they know to do so does not give a full or accurate assessment. We talk about "rose-colored glasses" worn by infatuated couples, but all too often, married people wear "contempt-colored glasses" that color everything in reverse.

Cherishing *can* conquer contempt, and one of its most potent weapons is thankfulness.

Thank You

To cherish isn't to merely look at a diamond, but to admire the way it sparkles and casts off the light. You're not just looking at it; you're delighting in its excellence and taking the time to notice its quality and superiority. A brief sidelong glance isn't cherishing. If there aren't any oohs and aahs, you're just looking to be polite. Cherishing thus means taking the time to notice and then to verbalize—either to yourself or others—its excellence.

While taking this time will spiritually feed our spouses and our marriages, it will also spiritually feed us. An interesting study described in *Psychology Today* found that, in one sense, learning to cherish actually makes us happier. According to this study, the person who benefits most from gratitude is the person who expresses it:

> Studies show that we can deliberately cultivate gratitude, and can increase our well-being and happiness by doing so. In addition, gratefulness—and especially expression of it to others—is associated with increased energy, optimism, and empathy.[13]

Active cherishing—noticing and then expressing the excellence you see—is a way to shape our attitudes and to generate feelings of closeness and well-being. When we do what the Bible tells us to do, we will be doubly blessed—our spouses will be happier, increasing the joy in our marriages, and we'll become happier psychologically as well. Cherishing our spouses literally makes us feel better.

So cherishing means waging war on contempt and going on the offense with gratitude.

How to Demotivate Your Spouse

Let's apply this science practically. My wife excels in so many ways, but one area she wishes she could excel in even more is getting me to consume less sugar. If you were to ask her one thing to change about me, I'm confident she'd say, "Get him to eat less sugar."

Lisa has high standards here. So-called healthy cereals still constitute "sugar" to Lisa because "they turn into sugar in your stomach." Lisa's "dessert" of choice is 85 percent or more dark chocolate. It's my contention that 85 percent dark chocolate isn't dessert—it's healthy enough to be considered a meal. Put a salad next to it and you've got an entrée.

One day when we were traveling, I asked Lisa how she felt about her day: "It was pretty good. I didn't get any kale today, but other than that, it was fine."

I have never and will never evaluate a day based on whether I got my kale.

One Lent, I decided to forgo processed sugar. I wouldn't add sugar to my tea; I wouldn't drink soda or sweet tea or eat any dessert that one eats only because it's sweet—no cookies, no cake, no candy bars, etc. But I also decided to do a historical Lent where you get to cheat on Sunday (it was historically considered inappropriate to fast on a celebratory day like Sunday).

When I grabbed a milk chocolate one Sunday, Lisa sighed that disappointed sigh many wives master.

"What?" I asked. "It's Sunday!"

"I was just hoping you'd lose your taste for it."

She might as well have told me she was hoping I'd turn into a Peep by Easter.

"Besides, you said you were giving up sugar, but you still have chai tea—and the mix has sugar in it. You have carbs for breakfast, and that turns into sugar in your stomach."

Here's the danger of pushing your husband too far: this was profoundly demotivating for me, because in my admittedly sinful being, I think, *Even after doing what feels like something dramatic to me—giving up processed sugar for six days out of seven—I will never please her in this area, so it's foolish to keep trying.*

I wasn't giving up sugar for Lent to please Lisa—I know she is making some valid points, so this was about me and God and body stewardship as much as anything (I freely confess I'm a struggling sinner here). I also understand Lisa's heart. She really cares about this, and she has told others that part of her service to God and the church (don't laugh) is to help me live longer. Every time she challenges me, she does so out of concern, never out of malice, spite, or selfishness.

But from a motivating perspective as it relates to marriage, I want to warn wives that if your husband thinks he can't please you in a certain area—if, for instance, he finally goes to church but then you complain because he doesn't worship enthusiastically enough when he's there—you're liable to *de*motivate him. Instead of cherishing him for joining you at church, he's criticized for not being there in the right way. Instead of thanking him for taking two steps, you're criticizing him for not taking three.

As Dr. Julie Gottman points out, we make daily choices about whether we scan our spouses for something to praise them for or something to find fault with.[14] Even if it's a *legitimate* fault, wrongly applied, it can push both men and women further into that fault. Lisa has excelled as a wife, but in this instance, it felt like she completely diminished the six good days on which I was committed to eating much less sugar (because I was still consuming some "hidden" sugars), and my one day of relaxing my standards became the focus—a failure of one day, not a triumph of six.*

---

* In case you're wondering, Lisa *did* fully read and approve the use of this story—and she particularly liked the fact that I called my fondness for sugar part of my life as a "struggling sinner."

His Beautiful Bride

I'll never forget a fortysomething husband—someone I'd never met before—who talked enthusiastically to me about the joy of being married to a "gorgeous" wife. The way he talked about her (and his close friends later assured me he *always* talked about her that way) made me expect to find the kind of woman that artists dream of painting.

As he spoke, I saw this knowing look in the eyes of his friends that I didn't quite understand. They knew what I was about to find out.

The man's "gorgeous" wife walked up a few minutes later. Not wanting to be unkind, all I can say is that she looked rather like a "before" picture of a glamour shoot. Except for her teeth, her hair, her grooming, and the asymmetrical set of her eyes, I'm sure she'd be stunning.

To her husband, she was.

When the couple walked away, one of the other men simply said, "Yeah, we don't get it either."

Cherish may not make sense to people outside the marriage, but it certainly makes the partners happier within it. We protect our spouses and their reputation instead of showing contempt, even when others may not agree with us.

Choose to cherish.

◈ CHERISHING CHERISH ◈

- Cherishing is marked by protecting our spouses' sense of worth and value—finding meaning in their lives and vocations.

- Cherishing calls us to go to war against contempt.

- Because all of us marry less than perfect people, if we don't apply grace, our spouses' faults can lead us to disappointment, which leads to frustration, which leads to bitterness, which leads to contempt. That's what we call the "cycle of contempt."

- Dr. John Gottman calls contempt the single biggest threat to a marriage's survival and happiness.

- We should be more concerned about our relationship with our spouses than anyone else, never throwing them under the bus to protect a different relationship, but instead taking the hit to win their loyalty and gratitude.

- One of cherishing's most potent weapons is thankfulness.

- If we look at how far our spouses have to go instead of how far they've come, we can demotivate them from further growth.

Questions for Discussion and Reflection

1. Describe a scene—in your own marriage or in another's—when you saw contempt on full display. What happened? What was the end result?

2. Describe a moment in your marriage when you felt like one of you threw the other under the bus. Now describe a moment when one of you took the hit. Talk about how that one moment in time impacted the relationship going forward.

3. Carlos and Rosa's story reveals that in many disputes, both partners are failing to cherish and protect each other and both have legitimate claims. Talk about how marital disagreements can be better served by each partner looking at how they are, at any given moment, failing to protect their spouse. It doesn't have to be an "either/or"; many times it's a "both/and."

4. Is there another person whose approval you are prone to put above your marriage? Your kids? Parents? A friend? Ask your spouse if they can think of someone who tempts you to do this, and humbly consider their thoughts.

5. Since being thankful for our spouses makes us happier in our marriages, what can you do to remind yourself of this when you start to feel disappointed in your marriage?

6. Think about an area in which your spouse needs to grow. How can you encourage him or her about how far they've traveled instead of fixating on how far they still have to go?

CHAPTER 6

A Bride Made Beautiful

Cherishing teaches us to indulge our spouses and thus help heal their spiritual wounds

L aura Kates grew up the very definition of a Southern daddy's girl. She adored her father, and growing up in the South five decades ago meant getting dressed for his arrival home. Every school day during kindergarten, Laura would come home, take a nap, get dressed in her best clothes with white shoes and clean laces, and walk out to the corner. Her dad stopped on his way home (less than a block away), kissed her, put her in the car, and drove into the parking lot of their apartment building.

One day, it all came to a sudden and sad end. Without any explanation or warning, in what seemed like a typical day, Laura got up from her nap, put on a dress and her little white shoes, and waited on the sidewalk.

Her dad never showed up.

After a while, Laura's mom came out and said maybe it was best for her to come inside, but Laura wouldn't budge. "I didn't want to disappoint him," she remembers. "I didn't want him to drive by and not see me waiting for him."

Finally, she had to go in, but she didn't go far. She parked herself right next to the living room window, where she could see the parking lot. Though she didn't stay at the window, her "vigil" lasted for years.

Over the rest of her life, Laura saw her father just two other times—and one of those times was a week before he died (Laura was then sixteen). She never got an adequate explanation. As an adult, she now knows there wasn't one, but the uncertainty was brutally troublesome for the dressed-up girl in her fancy dress who lived to see her father smile at the end of every workday.

When Laura married her husband, Curt, she told him, "I don't care how much money you make, what kind of house we live in, or how important your job is. I just want to be cherished."

Not surprisingly, for Laura being cherished means Curt *coming home*. "My highlight every day," Laura told me, her eyes getting misty even after almost four decades of marriage, "is when I hear the garage door open and I know my man is coming home to me."

Regarding the days when Curt and Laura were young, Laura says, "Most of our friends were in that upward and onward mode of work, but Curt chose time with me and our family over a superstar career. That's been huge for me. My husband said, 'I won't work until eight at night. I'm going home to my family.' We weren't as focused on a big paycheck as some of our peers were. Sadly, a lot of those couples are divorced. We're not rich like everybody else, but I don't care. Every night when I hear the garage door open, my heart starts racing because my man is coming back."

Laura and Curt model how a marriage marked by cherishing can heal the wounds with which we enter marriage. A cherishing marriage nurtures our souls and, as we'll see in Laura's continuing story near the end of this chapter, can lift us from broken neglect to dynamic impact.

A Pitiful Baby

There's a profound story in Ezekiel 16, when God tells Jerusalem that, though he found her in a pitiable state, he saved her, nurtured her, and cherished her to a heart-stopping glory. This chapter gives a picture of God's cherishing heart. We see his passion and care for his bride, Jerusalem. He demonstrates what it means to truly cherish someone others have neglected.

Using one of the most powerful word pictures in all of Scripture, Jerusalem is likened to an unwanted and abandoned infant, covered in the muck of birth and "left to die" (Ezekiel 16:5 NLT). The umbilical cord wasn't even cut (16:4 NIV); she wasn't "washed with water to make you clean, nor were you rubbed with salt or wrapped in cloths. No one looked on you with pity or had compassion . . . for you. Rather, you were thrown out into the open field, for on the day you were born you were despised" (16:4–5 NIV).

In the ancient Near East, washing and clothing a baby granted that child legitimacy. Ancient parents could cast off an unwanted child simply by failing to care for it immediately following birth, treating it as illegitimate.

This is a heartbreaking picture: even the child's parents don't want her. She is completely alone, unwanted, discarded—*despised*.

Hollywood romantic comedies make their money finding

new ways for couples to "meet cute"—they get in a minor car accident; they are businesspeople with opposing interests; one spills coffee on the other at a coffee shop. Ezekiel gives a scenario that is the opposite of meeting cute. It is meeting as ugly as ugly gets.

Jerusalem was cast off, ignored, helpless, grotesque in the muck of birth. Though today Jerusalem is one of the most famous cities in the world and indeed in world history, this is true only because God's cherishing love made her so. She was once anonymous, alone, unloved, and left to die, but then God came into the picture: "Then I passed by and saw you kicking about in your blood, and as you lay there in your blood I said to you, 'Live!' I made you grow like a plant of the field" (Ezekiel 16:6–7).

A good marriage, if we cherish each other as God cherished Jerusalem, is to proclaim to our spouses, *"Live!"* We see them in their very weakness, and even occasional ugliness, breathe life into each other and refresh each other. Dormant parts of our spouses' personalities and giftings can come alive under our support and encouragement.

Too many marriages instead breathe death—death to self-esteem, death to peace, death to joy. Our disappointment leads us to attack each other for what we're not, while cherishing grows the best parts of our giftings into their full power and adornment. A good marriage, a cherishing marriage, says to each partner, "Live! Come alive! Be all that God made you to be!"

That's what happened when God cherished Jerusalem. Then he proposes marriage to her (Ezekiel 16:7–8). Many marriages at that time, of course, were arranged—but not this one. This is a "love" marriage that God seeks out himself. Nobody told God to marry Jerusalem; he chose her.

Ezekiel now describes exactly how God cherishes his new bride by *indulging* her:

> "I . . . put ointments on you. I clothed you with an embroidered dress and put sandals of fine leather on you. I dressed you in fine linen and covered you with costly garments. I adorned you with jewelry: I put bracelets on your arms and a necklace around your neck, and I put a ring on your nose, earrings on your ears and a beautiful crown on your head. So you were adorned with gold and silver; your clothes were of fine linen and costly fabric and embroidered cloth. Your food was honey, olive oil and the finest flour."

> EZEKIEL 16:9–13

This is one spoiled spouse! She doesn't shop at Walmart; she wears Gucci and Armani, and she walks in Jimmy Choo shoes. When our youngest daughter traveled with us to Houston, we visited one of Houston's famous upscale malls, where a Jimmy Choo store can be found. Coming from the northern reaches of Washington state, young Kelsey was used to a very different kind of mall. "You mean Jimmy Choo shoes are real?" she asked. "I kind of thought they were just an urban legend."

Yes, they are real. And while our family would never buy them, God's bride, Jerusalem, certainly wore the equivalent.

Being cherished by God meant that Jerusalem was not only dressed lavishly but fed generously. She doesn't eat a dirty water hot dog from the sidewalk vendor; she gets to shop at the organic aisle of Whole Foods, where everything costs twice as much. The food is nurturing and tasty.

In short, God doesn't just provide for Jerusalem; he cherishes her, adorns her, nurtures her, and indulges her. When he told her to live, he was clearly intending her to live an *abundant* life (John 10:10).

Notice what this cherishing, this attentive care, did for Israel. It lifted her from a dependent baby left to die, neglected and despised, to become a stunningly beautiful, powerful, even regal woman envied by all: "You became very beautiful and rose to be a queen. And your fame spread among the nations on account of your beauty, because the splendor I had given you made your beauty perfect, declares the Sovereign LORD" (Ezekiel 16:13–14).

A later passage, Lamentations 2:15, at a different point in history, calls Jerusalem "the perfection of beauty, the joy of the whole earth."

God didn't cherish Israel because Israel was lovable; Israel became lovable as God cherished her. Cherish was the strategy God used to effect an enormous transformation in what Jerusalem became.

What was true of God toward Jerusalem is how we are to cherish each other in marriage. If marriage is about demonstrating God's character, our love for our spouses should be so intense, enthusiastic, and supportive that a similar transformation occurs. Can you get a vision for how your acceptance, commitment, and love for your spouse could lift him or her from a life of underachieving to one of glorious renown?

It can! God wants to exalt his children, and he is able, through his Holy Spirit, to do this for your spouse as you cooperate with him or her.

The biblical picture of God's love is perhaps best understood by the dumbfounded conversation of friends: "I don't know what he sees in her!" "What in the world does she see in him?"

They look at your commitment, and then they look at the object of your love—and they just don't get it. The person being cherished doesn't seem worthy of that kind of love and devotion—but since we take our cue from God, every Christian marriage should exhibit this kind of love and devotion.

To cherish as God cherished is to accept someone others may have rejected, to breathe life into them, to nurture them and spoil them, and even to indulge them until their beauty becomes evident for all to see.

Season Tickets

Remember Laura, the little girl whose father left her standing alone on the curb?

Today she is a beloved member at Second Baptist Church in Houston, Texas. She's an engaging Bible study teacher and enthusiastic friend. Part of Laura's forceful personality comes from losing a dad so young, from having to occasionally be the adult at a very early age, and from being naturally extroverted. All this—nature and nurture—has resulted in a "large and in charge" Texas girl with a Louisiana twist. Her slight frame harbors a giant personality.

She is "fully alive."

Just as God the Father cherished Jerusalem, so Curt, Laura's husband, has sought to cherish Laura—and not just by coming home on time. He looks for ways to indulge her.

One year, when the kids were young, Curt came up with a particularly brilliant idea.

Due to her father's abandonment, Laura lived her whole life hungering for but often deprived of beautiful things that enrich the soul. She and Curt had three small children at the time and couldn't get out much, but Curt splurged—spending probably more money than he should have—and bought season tickets to the Houston ballet.

They had gone to the ballet a couple times before, getting five-dollar dress rehearsal cheap seats through his company, and Curt noticed how much Laura loved it, so he bought a season package for two.

"He even bought good seats," Laura gushes, "*and* he went with me without grumbling."

If Curt had one hundred years' worth of free weekends and spent each one according to his wants, he'd never set foot in a ballet theater. Not even once. But giving his wife the tickets and going along with her meant something special to Laura and made her feel cherished: "It told me, 'Today, you are my priority.' It wasn't just that he gave me tickets; it's that he gave me himself."

When Curt handed Laura the tickets, he was thinking, *You're going to get to see the ballet.*

When Laura received the tickets, she was thinking, *He's committing to go on regular dates with me to something that I really love and that nourishes my soul.*

What Laura particularly appreciates about the way Curt cherishes her isn't the occasional gift (Curt admits he's usually not that good at giving gifts), but the way he makes Laura feel special for who she is. When your father has left you standing out on the curb, that's a healing place to be.

"I'm a strong person, but the fact that Curt lets me be me makes me feel especially cherished," Laura explains. "I'm the upfront person, the outgoing one. Some men might say, 'Hey, why should she be front and center all the time?' But Curt cherishes me for who I am. He lets me soar in those settings rather than fighting against me. For a man to let his wife be the shining one—that's special. And it encourages me to be the highest version of myself."

Like Jerusalem, Laura was once abandoned by her father. Like Jerusalem, she was chosen, cherished, and indulged, and has now become the highest version of herself—a queen in her realm, blessed by others and blessing others.

Curt has learned that cherishing Laura means letting her be on center stage in public, often the focus of attention, as God uses her (she's his ballerina; he's the partner stepping back into the shadows). It means he freely gives her the time to study to prepare her lessons or to invite people over for dinner. It means feeding her soul with occasional indulgences so she can be released in spirit with joy and vibrancy. It means agreeing to be alone at home while Laura is out speaking or on mission trips. It means being faithful to get home from work at a certain time.

Curt's cherishing actions have told his wife, "Live! Be who you are. I see now what others don't yet see—go and be that."

Through all of these actions, Curt has learned how to cherish the once-little girl who had her heart broken as she stood on the curb, wearing a fancy dress and stiff white shoes, to become a life-giving, Bible-teaching force of nature. He made a beautiful young woman yet more beautiful as a bride now approaching her fortieth wedding anniversary.

Go Ahead, Indulge Your Spouse

The way God cherished Jerusalem with such finery convinces me that if we truly cherish our spouses, there will be times when we will feel compelled to indulge them. I hate even the smell of prosperity theology (thinking that faith in God guarantees wealth, health, and happiness if we claim it in the right way and believe in it strongly enough); it repels me. But truth isn't found in reacting against error; it's found in responding to Scripture. And while we are called to be sacrificial and generous to the needy, here is an example of a husband's love compelling him to indulge his wife.

Nearly fifteen years ago, the Lord nudged Todd—a pastor of a midsize church with a young family and a tight budget—to be more intentional about cherishing his wife, Lisa. The problem was that Todd's plan would cost money—a challenge for his wife, who is the more frugal of the two.

Nevertheless, even knowing the risk and anticipating Lisa's pushback, Todd felt led by God to buy Lisa flowers every Friday for an entire year.

After just a few weeks, Lisa started to zero in on what was happening, and she told Todd (mainly because of the expense), "You know, you don't have to keep doing this."

Todd's response was, "Sorry, you don't get to weigh in on this one. It's something the Lord has asked me to do for you, so you'll need to take it up with him."

Todd calls that year "awesome" for his marriage. It set his heart in the right direction. It set a fantastic example for his sons. And it made an otherwise nondescript year of marriage stand out.

"Several times I had to be imaginative and creative. Once, Lisa went to the beach with her girlfriends. With the assistance of one of the women, I found out where they'd be eating and what time, and I had a bouquet of Gerbera daisies waiting at their table. Another time, I forgot it was a Friday until late at night, and I ended up making a literal eleventh-hour trip to get flowers from an all-night grocery store. On another occasion, we arrived at the beach for vacation on a Friday. Perfect. Once we got settled into our spot, the boys and I went to the store to find fresh flowers that Lisa could enjoy all week. Taking the boys with me gave me the opportunity to talk about why I was doing this."

This act of indulging his wife on a weekly basis in spite of a tight budget helped Todd pass down a generational commitment for their sons to cherish their wives. "I watched my dad cherish my mom time and time again when I was growing up, and I wanted my boys to see me do the same—to treat Lisa like she's something special. Even though I had seen a great example of a cherishing marriage while growing up, it was something I had begun to take for granted in my marriage. I think God just wanted to wake me up. Thankfully, I had an example to draw from—and a wife who could make the necessary budgetary adjustments to be cherished without worrying that I was breaking the bank."

Markers

Some of you married superstars—I've got a story about one such couple in a later chapter. But some of you married men and women who felt beat-up their entire lives, emotionally if not physically. What would our marriages look like if we responded with concern for our partner's character weaknesses by assuming they may (not always) have been maintained or even fed by our failure to cherish them? Instead of being frustrated about why they are the way they are, what if we assumed that their continued weakness may be evidence that we have failed to cherish them as we should, just as God cherished Jerusalem and lifted her up from a place of being abandoned to that of being a queen admired by the entire world?

Dennis and Barbara Rainey provide a helpful list of traits of spouses who don't feel cherished (they use the language of "low self-esteem," but it's a similar concept). If several of these things are present in your spouse, it may be that he or she doesn't feel cherished by you:

- Your mate gets discouraged easily.
- Your mate lacks confidence, especially in decision making.
- Your mate has difficulty admitting he or she is wrong and always needs to be right.
- Your mate is a driven person.
- Your mate is critical of others.
- Your mate is a perfectionist.
- Your mate is self-critical.
- Your mate indulges in escapism.[15]

There are, of course, limits to general principles, and it can be dangerous to take ownership of a spouse's sin. But for those annoying behaviors you see in your spouse, ask yourself, "Would these things be so annoying if I cherished him more?" In other words, instead of thinking, *Why must I put up with this?* cherish it out of him or her.

To Cherish Is to Heal

In short, cherishing can heal. To ridicule your spouse or to be apathetic about your spouse is to further injure them. Contempt merely reinforces the negativity from earlier in your spouse's life. You push her down lower and lower. Cherishing lifts her higher and higher. To not cherish is to reinforce the worst and make it worse yet. To cherish is to call out the beauty and to make what is latent yet more beautiful.

Just speaking practically, when my wife cherishes me, I want to be more of what she cherishes. Short of God's call and acceptance, nothing is more motivating to me than when my wife cherishes what I do.

I'm not alone in this. One wife gave her husband a journal she had worked on for an entire year. It listed everything she noticed about him throughout the year—mentioning specific things he had done on specific days—that made her glad to be married to him.*

- Thank you for hanging the Christmas lights when it was freezing outside. You want our family to have joy. It was so cold that it must have been terrible. I wouldn't have wanted to do that, but you did.
- Thank you for traveling. I know it must be hard. I could see how tired you were when you walked out the door on February 6. You do such a good job providing for our family.
- Thank you for coming home so tired from that trip in September but still eager to spend time with the children. You're such a good father.

When she gave him the journal, her husband immediately sat down in a chair and read the entire journal in one sitting. Later, when recounting this gift to a friend, he told him, "Reading that journal makes me aspire to be the man she thinks I am."

---

* I'm grateful to Dave and Ann Wilson (daveandannwilson.com) for sharing this story with me. Dave is the pastor of Kensington Church in Troy, Michigan. He and his wife, Ann, speak around the country on marriage.

Guess what? He now gets a journal like that *every year.*

A common complaint among wives is that their husbands won't open up, won't be vulnerable, won't emotionally give of themselves. The reality is that many guys are too terrified of being truly known. Some of us have been ridiculed all our lives because we weren't as smart as our older brother or sister, as athletic as the star football player who started shaving in sixth grade, as attractive as the members of the boy bands whose posters our sisters put on their bedroom walls—and we kind of figured out that we sometimes were just plain embarrassing to our family. Now we somehow—wonder of wonders—found a woman who chose us, and we don't want to risk losing her or it'll be yet one more rejection—like getting cut from a sports team, being let go at work, or getting seven rejections when applying to college or grad school.

Even those men who seem to succeed often feel like a failure. I've talked to them! They're worried they've been promoted so high that they'll finally be exposed. Everyone will realize it's all been a ruse; everyone has been tricked—and they are just the utter, insignificant failures that they've always felt they are and often been told they are.

Your spouse likely did not grow up in an affirming world. Kids are not kind to each other—on the contrary, they can destroy each other. Most women don't look like Barbie, and most men don't look like Hercules.

Let's say a boy grows up slight in stature (as God created him). He's belittled by a gruff father or mother, ridiculed by boys and girls alike. He becomes a man, no longer so slight, but still carrying the internal dialogue and slightly sensitive persona ingrained in him through years of ridicule and insecurity. God sees a hurting soul. God has cried over that poor boy's treatment, and God *hates* it when a woman who hasn't taken the time to understand or empathize says in a moment of cutting anger, "Oh, grow up and be a *man*."

It's a casual comment, perhaps not even intended to be so hurtful, but because of that guy's past, it cuts to the deepest part of his being. Oh, he may never tell his wife how much it hurts, but you can be sure he's bleeding, spiritually and emotionally, on the inside.

Never forget: You married a spouse with natural weaknesses. You married a spouse with a history of hurt. We can be agents of healing redemption and acceptance in our marriage, or we can do further harm, perhaps unintentionally. Though I'm sure the wife who said "grow up and be a man" would have been appalled to know how tough her words felt, what her husband likely heard was, "You haven't hurt *enough*. Those people who ridiculed you when you were a child? They were *right*! You're *pathetic*. You need to suffer *more*, and I'm just the person to do it."

She would *never* use those words to her man, but because of his past, that's what he's hearing. A casual, noncherishing comment, with just a dash of contempt, is digging up the old scripts from his childhood that now play back the same destructive, discouraging message: *you don't matter.*

You become a messenger of Satan instead of a servant of God when you unleash that, even unwittingly.

Why is your wife so sensitive to others' opinions? Why does your husband have such a difficult time making decisions? Why does your wife find comfort by slipping off by herself and eating food she knows is disgusting? Why does your husband find comfort in electronic fantasy?

Don't just tell me what your spouse does. Tell me why, and then we can talk about the pathway of love and healing.

If you don't know the why, you're just an accusing judge who knows nothing of love, only something of punishment.

I am not excusing sinful or abhorrent behavior. I'm just asking you to have some empathy about the fact that we live in a cruel world, vicious in its treatment of the people we marry, as well as a positive vision for how profoundly a cherishing marriage can heal past hurts. No, not every abused man grows up to abuse his wife. Not every woman allows herself to be crushed by others' ridicule; some become incredibly strong and heroic in the face of their pasts.

But here's the thing: *Why not help your spouse get stronger by cherishing them rather than confirming and increasing their weakness by treating them with contempt?* Wouldn't you rather be married to someone who is improving rather than sliding backward? And do you think contempt is "medicine" for a warped psyche that sees the world through perverted eyes?

What if you took the long-term view? "I've got twenty to fifty more years to gradually cherish this man or woman out of their past hurt and weakness." Does it sound so impossible then?

What does contempt heal? Who does contempt call into becoming a better person? What does contempt have to do with grace? Anything?

Some of you need to repent right now and then ask for your spouse's forgiveness. You have ridiculed your partner's limitations (let's be honest, some of these limitations—IQ, body type, personality—are there by God's design), and you have increased their hurt. You are pushing them down instead of lifting them up. You resent them for not being where you want them to be instead of getting on your knees to help them grow in ways God would have them grow.

Stop it.

Note that the biblical model of cherishing is basically the reverse of the world's model. In the world, cherishing in marriage flows out of a spouse's excellence: "I cherish you because you're so wonderful." The biblical model is rather, "Your excellence flows out of my cherishing you."

This is why I call cherishing a strategy as much as a command. The more you cherish, the more likely there will be even more to cherish in the future. The more you pour contempt into your marriage, the less you will find to cherish.

Will you please do yourself and your spouse a favor? Spend time in prayer during the next twenty-four hours, asking God to show you just how empty, tired, and beat-up your spouse felt at the beginning of your relationship because of the way they had been treated for decades before they arrived in your arms.

Exhausted

The finish line of a marathon can be quite an ugly place. When I cross the finish line, I want two things: something to drink and somewhere to sit or lie down. When Lisa guides me to a place where I can rest and brings me something to rehydrate, I slowly become a new man.

It's the best description of cherishing I can give you: I'm exhausted, at the end of myself, but with my wife's loving care, bringing me a little hydration, a little protein, a little rest, I feel the life coming back into me.

Consider marriage to be like the end of a marathon, and you'll begin to get a glimpse at how depleted emotionally your husband or wife may have been as you began your marriage. That's how thirsty he or she was for your affection. That's how much he or she wanted to just lie down in your acceptance.

Become the most wonderful wife in the world by telling him—with your attention, your affection, and your acceptance—"You've made it across the finish line into my arms. I'm yours, and you are mine. We're one. I'm thrilled with you. I love you. You can rest in my acceptance. I will recharge you with my affection. I won't pull away when I get to know you; I'll draw closer. I won't disrespect you when I find the dark within you; I'll pray for God to flood you with his light. I won't compare you to any other man because to me you are the only man of my affections; you are the standard; you are my man of all men. I won't look at another man; I won't touch another man; I won't compare you to any other man. I will feast my eyes and fill my heart with my love for you."

Men, when your wife faces a major life blow—she becomes seriously sick, finds out she can't conceive, suddenly struggles with weight gain, is fighting depression for the first time in her life, can't get over the sense that it feels impossible to balance her career and her parenting—these are the exact moments when you need to put cherish on overdrive. We have to say, "Now is the time she truly needs the medicine of cherish." Instead of pulling back in disgust—"I want a healthy and happy wife, not a broken one!"—we need to step forward with cherish. If you fail to cherish your wife in the difficult times, the damage done by those difficulties will be twice as bad and take three times as long to heal.

As God the Father cherished Jerusalem, so we are to cherish each other. That means nurturing each other, breathing life into each other, indulging each other, and continuing to choose each other.

CHERISHING CHERISH

- Just as God the Father cherished Jerusalem, so we are to cherish our spouses.

- A godly marriage breathes life into each partner.

- Cherishing a spouse can lift them from the hurts and wounds of their childhood and help them achieve the full splendor of who God made them to be.

- Cherishing is a strategy. God didn't cherish Israel because Israel was lovable; Israel became lovable as God cherished her. Cherish was the strategy God used to bring about an enormous transformation.

- What would our marriages be like if we expressed concern for our partners' character weaknesses by assuming they may have been either fed or maintained by our failure to cherish them? Instead of being frustrated about why they are the way they are, what if we assumed that their continued weakness may be evidence that we have failed to cherish them as we should?

- Many people feel emotionally beat-up by the time they get married. Cherishing can bring healing; contempt only increases childhood injury.

Questions for Discussion and Reflection

1. How does considering God's love for Jerusalem challenge you to become a more cherishing spouse?

2. How can a cherishing marriage breathe life into each partner?

3. Laura feels most cherished every day when she hears the garage door open and knows Curt is coming home. What hurts from your spouse's past can you gently "cherish away" by being faithful in some little thing?

4. Can you identify any character weaknesses in your spouse that you believe could be at least lessened if they felt more intensely cherished by you? Describe how.

5. Without consulting your spouse, write a description of how beat-up and exhausted you think they must have felt when they met you. Show the list to your spouse and ask if you are correct. Ask them to add to it. Knowing this, how do you want to treat them in the coming days?

CHAPTER 7

I Almost Quit

We've already covered a lot of ground, so let's pause for a brief devotional thought. If you think your marriage is beyond all that we've talked about—that there's just no way you could go from contempt to cherishing, consider this.

My mother-in-law recently stunned me by reminding me of a long-forgotten conversation. Just six years into my marriage with Lisa, I told her parents, "I think it may be time to just give up."

I wasn't talking about my marriage; I was talking about my writing career.

"It's costing us money we don't have," I explained, "and now that kids are in the picture, it's costing me time I don't have. I gave it a good shot, but maybe it's just not going to happen."

More than twenty years later, within a week of that conversation with my mother-in-law, I signed the largest publishing contract of my life, for an additional four books, after having already published eighteen.

I shuddered when my mother-in-law told me I almost quit twenty years ago. I can't imagine any other life than what I've had, and the thought that I once seriously contemplated letting it go—just because it was harder and taking me longer than I thought it should—chills me to my very core.

One woman told me the painful story of her mother who quit on her marriage. She got fed up and married another man—and then her ex-husband got serious about the Lord. "Today, he's the most amazing man," his daughter said. "He's secure financially, and my mom is now married to an unbeliever who doesn't provide very well, so she's working a menial job even though she's in her sixties. What's saddest is that she lived with my dad through his *worst* years, but because she quit she missed his *best* years."

How many couples do that? How many suffer through their worst years, get frustrated and quit, and miss out on what could be their best years?

When times are really tough, when a dream seems ridiculously deferred so you feel foolish for even continuing to believe, it's easy to let it all slip away and say, "Enough is enough." The present is so painful, so disappointing, that you are blinded to a future that's even marginally better, much less stupendously so.

Of course, there's no promise that if you persevere, you'll get just what you're hoping for. But the one certainty is that if you give up, you definitely *won't* get it. If your dream is a life-long love, a lifelong marriage, and you end it, you will never have a life shared with just one other person. Life is real, and sometimes the process of real life can be so heartbreaking, so disappointing, or just so underwhelming that you can't imagine it will ever change.

But it can, and it often does.

Have you ever thought about what made the *Rocky* movies so successful? It wasn't the fight scenes. Those were melodramatic, bordering on the comic. Nobody could take the beatings meted out in those battles. What lifted *Rocky* above so many movies is that Sylvester Stallone brilliantly featured Rocky Balboa's *day-to-day training*, with Bill Conti's magnificent song, "Gonna Fly Now," playing in the background.

That daily reality of the persistent, anonymous struggle is what resonated with people, what inspired them, what made their aspirations soar. It wasn't the end result—Rocky lost the first bout, after all; it was the process that made the movies so interesting.

The same is true in marriage. Without struggle, marriage is like melodrama. If God allowed infatuation to remain, how many of us would do the day-to-day work to achieve real intimacy?

When I see an infatuated couple now, I see melodrama, and I don't envy them. I know they will have to face the moment when their eyes are really and truly opened. Then they will have to fight disappointment; some may even find themselves battling contempt. They smile now and kiss each other's hands, but they have a lot of work ahead of them in the near future—and frankly, I'm glad I'm on the other side.

Here's what so many couples don't realize because it's *never* featured in the movies (which focus exclusively on the melodrama of infatuation): there's something even better than infatuation—cherishing someone you truly know.

I've been infatuated, and I've lived cherish.

Cherish is better.

It takes work to get to a cherishing marriage. It requires accepting the day-to-day training rather than pining for the melodramatic fight scene in front of the crowds. But in the end, cherishing is what will carry the movie.

Before you quit on a frustrating relationship, realize that infatuation has to die before authentic intimacy (knowing and accepting) can actually begin. Learning how to cherish is the road map to give an old relationship fresh wind, new hopes, and better days.

Don't feel foolish for continuing to believe. Consider yourself an unknown boxer from Philly who is being given a surprising shot at notoriety, waking up early, drinking raw eggs, chasing chickens, and doing everything he must do to achieve his dream.

That morning in California, visiting my mother-in-law, I was delighted to be with Lisa. I cherished her. I put my arm around her shoulder. I wanted to hold her hand and make sure I kissed her good-bye when I returned to the hotel to work as she prepared to spend the day with her mom. If you had told me on my wedding day that this is what my marriage would look and feel like thirty years in, I would have said, "Cool!" But if you had said that to me during certain seasons of our marriage, I may not have believed you. In moments of desperation, it's difficult to see hope in the distant future.

If I could go back and speak to that twenty-eight-year-old me, I'd say, "Hang in there, Gary. It's still not near. You've got another four years before things really break for your writing. But when they do, the joy of what you'll have will swallow up the pain of what you don't, tenfold."

I believe the same can be true for you in marriage.

Please don't quit.

CHAPTER 8

Cherishing Words

Cherishing teaches us to carefully and deliberately use our ears and our words to express our affection

Lisa thought she had met a near-perfect man sitting next to her on an airplane, until he talked himself into the gutter. She figures he was a doctor, given what he looked at on his computer and the paper he was writing. What really got her excited, however, was the food he brought with him on the plane. "He was super healthy," Lisa recounted with enthusiasm. "He drank a green smoothie, had a bottle of seltzer water, and ate a quinoa-and-black-bean salad, a bagful of carrots, and a chunk of cheddar cheese for dessert."

If you knew my wife, you would know this is as attractive as it gets. If "you are what you eat," Lisa loves someone who eats healthy.

On that same flight (we booked late and couldn't get two seats together), Lisa's husband (that would be me) ate a yogurt parfait ("Do you realize how much sugar is in that kind of yogurt?" Lisa asked me), a bag of nuts, and some dark chocolate raisins (the "dark" part matters to Lisa—a marital compromise between the two of us).

How could I compete for esteem with a guy who chooses a green smoothie when his wife isn't even with him, actually purchases a quinoa-and-black-bean salad, and considers a chunk of cheddar cheese "dessert"?

After we landed, Lisa heard the doctor take a phone call, and her opinion about him completely changed. In clipped tones, he was cruelly short with his wife; there was no "warm-up," no endearing "hello, sweetie"—just a hard utilitarianism: "Yeah. Okay, well, I'm still on the plane . . . Whatever." After several phrases like this, his voice suddenly changed: "Hiiiiii Alex, how are yooooouuuu?"

Then it changed back again for the worse: "Okay. That's fine."

"I already *said* we can go as soon as I get home."

"Fine."

"Bye."

The absence of any "it's good to hear your voice," "I love you," or enthusiasm (like he showed for his child) made it a pretty cold call. He cherished his kid with his voice, but not his wife.

This doctor, given his training and his practice of medicine, understands far more about the human body than I could ever hope to learn. He may treat diseases with the best of them. But did he realize the damage this simple phone call did to his marriage? Did he realize the climate he was creating for his soon-to-be marital reunion?

"What was the matter with what I said?" he might argue.

But that's the wrong question if you are seeking to cherish. Cherish is something positive, not the lack of negative. To cherish, you have to ask, "What was *right, affirming, loving* about that conversation?"

Every conversation—every one!—takes you closer to or farther away from a cherishing marriage. The Bible declares this truth: "The tongue has the power of life and death" (Proverbs 18:21). I love the way Barbara and Dennis Rainey describe this: "We can create life in our mates with our positive words, or we can inflict destruction with our negative or neglectful words."[16]

Donnie freely admits he "lives and dies by verbal affirmation." That was a problem when he fell in love with Jaclyn, who grew up in a home where people almost never even said "I love you."

After reading *The Five Love Languages* together, Jaclyn was a bit concerned when she found out that Donnie's strongest love language, by far, is words of affirmation. "I'm just not good at that," she told him.

But Jaclyn wanted Donnie to feel cherished, so she began writing out things she could praise him for, as well as things she liked about him. That initial list ended up running almost five pages.

Once Jaclyn got started, she couldn't stop. Nearly a dozen years into their marriage, Donnie feels deeply cherished. "She's such an encouragement to me," he says.

What touches Donnie as much as Jaclyn talking to him is when he hears her telling another family member—Jaclyn's grandmother, for instance—about something wonderful he has just done.

Theirs is an important lesson: if we want our spouses to feel cherished, we may have to work at a few things we're not so good at by nature. Words are too powerful a tool not to put into service if we want a cherishing marriage.

Early on in their marriage, Jaclyn heard a woman tell her, "Never say a bad word about your husband."

"That was huge to me," Jaclyn says. "Where I grew up, men were losers, and women had to wear the pants. Every wife I knew talked badly about her husband. I'm so glad a woman told me that marriage didn't have to be like that, that we didn't have to talk about each other that way. That kind of negative talk would have been so hurtful to Donnie if I had decided to act like the wives I had seen while growing up."

One of the other ways that Jaclyn and Donnie have learned to use words to serve a cherishing purpose is to keep their sexual desire for each other at a high level. "We have a ton of inside jokes," she says. "We can turn *anything* into a sexual reference. Of course, we don't do that in front of anyone else, but it's always something that makes us laugh."

Donnie and Jaclyn have learned to excel at using words as tools to help each other feel cherished.

Curiosity Saved the Marriage

Pam Farrel writes in several of her books that a wife often feels most loved when her husband is simply more *curious* about her.[17] If a husband says, "I want to know *more*," for some women, that's straight-out verbal foreplay. It gets them really excited emotionally.

"My husband is interested in me. He wants to hear more. Not only am I not boring him; he can't get enough of me."

And I'm sure this is equally true for beaten-down husbands who are rarely respected at home or work.

But notice how this is based on initiating. It's not enough to simply listen. We have to take the next step, engage, and go even further to say, "I want more. Tell me more." *We have to maintain our curiosity.*

Isn't this partly what made dating so intoxicating? To hear someone say, "Tell me all about you. What do you think? What do you do? What have you been through? I want to hear more"? Suddenly, we were no longer invisible. A woman or a man seemed fascinated by our past and eager to get to know us in the present. For many of us, such conversations made us come alive. After years of being dismissed by parents and older siblings, countless peer groups, and the general apathy of a self-absorbed world, someone made us feel like we mattered and had something worthwhile or at least interesting to say. (This is also how many stories of infidelity begin. When you feel neglected by your spouse and someone else becomes curious, it can hit your numbed soul like a drug.)

While Jaclyn learned to use words to affirm Donnie, Donnie had to learn how to use his ears and even his eyes to affirm his curiosity. "A teacher once told me you listen with your eyes as much as your ears. If you want someone to feel like you care, you have to look at them."

Donnie applies this with Jaclyn. "I make sure I start looking at her as soon as she starts talking. That helps me to focus. Even if I'm not particularly interested in what she's saying, I'm still interested in the person who is talking, so I'm looking at her."

One time, while Donnie was trying to wrap up a potential $200,000 project due the next morning, Jaclyn found herself talking about something she had read on Facebook about an old friend. In truth, Donnie couldn't have cared less about that person *at that moment*. He was totally focused on a time-urgent work task.

But because Donnie cherishes Jaclyn, he looked up at her and listened. "I didn't care about that friend as much as I cared about the $200,000 project, but I care about Jaclyn *more* than I care about the $200,000 project, so I stopped what I was doing and listened."

Husbands, cherishing often isn't about what your wife is saying; it's about who is saying it. Donnie's attitude could serve as a lesson for us all.

Pursue Me

Let me speak a bit more about how curiosity creates and maintains a cherishing marriage. My wife and I were at a women's book group that had just read *Sacred Influence* together and wanted to discuss it with us. One woman asked a very fair question: "Why do wives read half a dozen marriage books for every one book our husbands read?"

Men, if you want to cherish your wife as Christ cherishes the church, cherishing with curiosity means you have to at least occasionally be the initiator, as Christ was the initiator in his relationship with the church. We were estranged from God, so Jesus came to us to bring us back. He didn't wait for the church to approach him. He didn't expect that the bride, as the "relational" one, would be more invested in the relationship and plead with him to come back.

If you cherish your wife with curiosity, there will be times when *you* are the one who says those famous words, "We need to talk." *You* will be the one who researches the best marital counselor if one is needed. You may even ask your wife to go to a marriage conference with you instead of waiting for her to invite you. If your wife feels like she's the only one trying to improve your marriage, then you're not curious, and you're not cherishing her.

Now a quick word to women: If curiosity, in the right way and with the right tone, makes your man feel cherished, you'll also initiate some conversations. Some women may be wary to ask their husbands what they think, believing they already know all they need to know or are sure they'll disagree. Perhaps they assume that seeking their husband's opinion is akin to seeking his permission—and anything that smacks of submission is to be sneered at as an egregious relic from the barbaric past. Just know this, wives: If your husbands never hear you seeking their opinion, the main conclusion they will draw is that their opinion doesn't matter to you. And in that climate, your husband will never feel cherished.

Men and women, if you have an important business client, you make it your business to know what they are doing and who might be courting them—you maintain your curiosity or risk losing the relationship. In a sense, marriage is similar. Apathy in marriage is one of the worst wounds a spouse can inflict.

Dietrich Bonhoeffer calls listening one of the greatest services we can offer to each other:

> The first service one owes to others in the fellowship consists in listening to them. Just as love to God begins with listening to His Word, so the beginning of love for the brethren is learning to listen to them . . . So it is His work that we do for our brother when we learn to listen to him . . . Listening can be of a greater service than speaking.[18]

This means if you want to cherish your spouse, you have to live by James 1:19 and be "quick to listen" and "slow to speak." Cherishing requires an eager ear and a strategic tongue. It means maintaining our curiosity.

This Way, Hon

Now that we're empty nesters, Lisa travels with me on most of my trips. I had to figure out all over again what it means to cherish Lisa verbally when we travel. That's what marriage is—continually evolving as a couple as your lives change. Otherwise you'll grow apart instead of together.

In this new season of joint travel, Lisa had an uncanny ability to always turn right out of the elevator when she should have turned left. We got into a parking lot, and she invariably turned north when the car was south. Lisa has a tenuous relationship with time—the clock has its opinion and Lisa has hers—so we usually found ourselves rushing a bit to leave; no doubt she was distracted. And when we returned from somewhere, Lisa was so focused on recounting a conversation or talking to me that she just didn't bother to even try to remember where our room or car was. She knew I knew the way, so she just kept talking.

The first couple times Lisa turned the wrong way, I thought it was a simple mistake. Finally, after several times (we had been there a couple days), I said, "Seriously? Again?"

That didn't work so well (you can imagine), so the next time, I simply turned in the right direction and waited for Lisa to notice.

That didn't work so well either.

"So what am I supposed to do?" I asked her. "If I say nothing, you get upset. If I mention it's the wrong way, you say it makes you feel stupid. I'm at a loss here."

"It's so easy," Lisa said. "Just say a simple 'this way, hon' in *exactly that tone.*

So the next time, that's what I did.

"This way, hon."

Lisa turned and smiled a gorgeous smile. "Perfect," she said.

Now we laugh whenever that happens. It draws us closer together rather than slowly pulling us apart. It's become part of our marital story.

Words really matter to most spouses, and tone is a big part of it. Your spouse won't feel cherished if you don't learn to control your tone.

But notice, sometimes you have to ask your spouse how to cherish them in moments when they don't feel cherished. I had been married to Lisa for thirty years, but I still had to ask her, "Okay, you tell me—how do I redirect you without hurting you?" A wife may have to ask her husband, "How can I disagree with you or offer a contrary opinion without making you feel like I don't respect you?"

Verbal slights that are often unintentional can drain the life out of your marriage. Perhaps you could ask your spouse— particularly if you're reading this with him or her right now—whether there is a similar situation in your relationship where you need to learn to say, "This way, hon."

For instance, it took me a couple decades to learn how to wake up Lisa. Early on, I was confused as a husband. When I woke her up at the appointed time, she seemed angry at me for disturbing her sleep. When I let her sleep in, she was angry that I didn't wake her up. I felt like I couldn't win.

But when I learned how to gently and slowly wake her up, how to essentially "cherish" her awake, that all changed. I had set it up so *she* was the problem: whether I woke her up or let her sleep in, I was in trouble. But the issue was actually the *way* I was doing it. Now, if I'm going to be home in the morning, Lisa never wants to set her clock because, she says, "You're so much more pleasant than an alarm clock."

Be Specific and Deliberate

Deliberately choosing the way we speak is essential to a lifetime of cherishing our mates. The early church father John Chrysostom urged husbands (speaking about their wives), "Never call her by her name alone, but with terms of endearment also, with honor, with much love. If you honor her, she won't require honor from others; she won't desire that praise that others give if she enjoys the praise that comes from you. Prefer her before all others, in every way, both for her beauty and for her sensitivity, and praise her."[19]

Cherishing calls us to be specific. As a young husband, I failed to understand how much of my adoration of Lisa was missed by her and how much of my disappointment was caught. I'd think to myself, *Wow, Lisa looks fantastic!* but when I didn't say it, Lisa would think, *He isn't saying anything. It must be a bad hair day.*

Silence is often unintentionally malicious, so try to verbalize every positive thing you can think of. And that means being specific. It means so much more to Lisa when I say, "Your eyes are all lit up and gorgeous tonight!" than a general "you look great." (Although I don't think she's ever hated hearing "you look great.")

Why are you enamored with your spouse? What do you admire about your spouse? What makes you smile when you think about your spouse?

Tell her.

Tell him.

When we criticize ourselves or others criticize us, we and they tend to be extremely specific: "It drives me crazy when you crack your knuckles." "You're a slob; look at this mess." "You're lazy and you never get off the couch." Using specific words of authentic praise counteracts this. As Barbara and Dennis Rainey put it, "Your praise can be excessive only if your words are insincere. Genuine, heartfelt praise cannot be overdone."[20]

If you don't speak encouraging words to your spouse, who will? I love the way the Raineys put this obligation on the plate of every married partner: "You have the main responsibility for sowing words of belief and admiration in your spouse."[21] No farmer expects a neighbor, distant relative, or church member to sow the seed in his field; it's his farm, and therefore his responsibility. As soon as you get married, it is no longer your in-laws' job to be your spouse's main encourager (something is wrong if that's the case); it is not your children's job; it is not your church group's job or your spouse's employer's job. It is not even your spouse's best friend's job. It is *your* job to be your spouse's chief advocate, encourager, and cherisher.

Are you doing your job?

One weekend, thirty years into our marriage, I had one of those brutal travel days. I spoke at a graduation ceremony for the Sacramento branch of Western Seminary on a Saturday morning and planned to immediately fly back to Houston to preach at the eleven o'clock service on Sunday morning for Second Baptist.

That's an appointment with roughly five thousand people.

As soon as the ceremony was over, I got a text from United Airlines: my first flight was delayed, which meant I'd miss my connection into Houston. I called the airline in near desperation: "You've got to get me back to Houston before tomorrow morning."

The customer service rep said, "We can reroute you through San Francisco. You can catch an 11:15 p.m. flight into Houston, arriving at 5:15 in the morning."

"I'll take it."

I spent about nine hours total at two different airports, tried to grab a few moments of sleep once I got on the 11:15 flight, and, after landing and picking up my bags, made it back to my house four hours before the church service began. I laid down for an unproductive two hours of wishful slumber and then showered and shaved and made it to the church on time.

It was a surreal feeling to stand on a stage in front of five thousand people in Houston when I had been sitting in a San Francisco airport ten hours earlier in the dead of night.

Later that day, my wife posted on Facebook:

> In awe of my husband today . . . he arrived home at 7am after nine hours of flight delays, got out of bed CHEERFULLY at 9 (thankful for his two hours of sleep), and preached a great sermon at 11! And he even looked good, without the benefit of makeup or coffee :).

Frankly, she had me at "awe." When a wife says something like that publicly, I don't even need to hear what follows. I felt cherished. I felt ten feet tall. I expected to look in the mirror and see a full head of hair.

That's the power of affirming words.

Keep in mind that whenever you affirm something, that trait or quality is usually reinforced: "I appreciate your integrity; I love your joy; your kindness is so amazing." It tends to increase the good. When a spouse thinks, *I guess I am kind*, he is likely to want to keep acting in a kind manner, because that's how he sees himself. That becomes part of his identity. If you want to see change in your spouse, find a kernel of something good and reinforce it specifically and verbally. Remember the husband whose wife gave him the journal of all his most excellent acts throughout the year? Do you remember how he responded? "Reading that journal makes me aspire to be the man she thinks I am."

In one sense, affirming your spouse is a spiritual as well as a marital duty. Author Sam Crabtree opens his book *Practicing Affirmation* with a strong statement: "If God is sovereign, and every good gift is from above, then not praising the good in others is kind of a sacrilege and soul-sickness."[22] One of the ways we worship God is to pause long enough to examine his work, not just in painting a sunset, but in giving a formerly anger-ridden man a little more patience and kindness or acknowledging that a once impatient woman now displays the perseverance of Job. Acknowledge the growth. Proclaim it. Praise it.

Be Soft

At this point, it should be understood that abusive speech has no place—*none*—in a marriage based on cherishing each other. To explode verbally against your spouse, to berate your spouse, to ridicule your spouse, to wound your spouse with words— all of this is the opposite of what marriage is supposed to be. Colossians 3:19 (NRSV) gives a fuller picture of what cherishing means when it provides a concise and succinct recipe to men as to how to cherish their wives. Paul tells husbands to "love your wives and never treat them harshly."

Can you find a clearer command in all of Scripture?

Always choose to love.

Never treat them harshly.

To treat your wife harshly means engaging in any action that makes life feel bitter to her. Harsh is the exact opposite of cherish. This passage is essentially telling men, "Since you are called to cherish your wives, never do the opposite of cherish, which is being harsh."

If you are harsh with your wife—certainly physically, but also verbally, emotionally, or even intellectually (in the way you think about her)—you haven't even stepped onto the sacred path of cherishing. You have to decide that just as a true patriot would never take up arms against his own country—he would sooner die first—so you won't attack your spouse in any way. It must be unthinkable, in the realm of the impossible.

Your fists will never punch her, though they might form to protect her. Your tongue will speak hard truth at times, but only to heal, encourage, and release the light—never to demean, to ridicule, to harm. Your arms and your affection are the steadiest, warmest, most comfortable part of her human, earthbound existence. Surrounded by you, she knows you will take the first blow.

Men, it's a really bad sign—telling you that something has gone seriously wrong—if your wife ever defines her marital experience as bitter. That's the opposite of cherish.

Women can also be verbally violent, of course. Now that our friends are parents of kids who are getting married, we see marriage from a different angle—how our children are treated by their spouses. One of our friends has several sons, and it hurts her when she sees one of her daughters-in-law speak harshly to her son.

"The reality is, my son just doesn't see the trash she wants him to pick up. He's not intentionally trying to be messy; he's just blind to it. But when he forgets to pick it up and then maybe leaves the garage door open at night, his wife tells him, 'You can't do anything right. I can't trust you with *anything*.'

"That kind of language just kills him. And I'm so afraid it's just going to make him give up."

I asked our friend, "So what should your son's wife do differently? How can she speak more softly?"

"There's tremendous power in the word *babe*. It softens everything that follows. 'Hey, babe, you left the garage door open again. Please be a little more careful.' That one word sets an entirely different tone: 'you're not my enemy; you're still my babe.' But it has to be more than just addressing the negative in a positive way. Speak life into your husband; speak words of encouragement; respect him with your words; notice the little things and thank him."

Her husband broke into the conversation: "Noticing is *huge*."

The wife smiled and added, "Never forget that your twenty- or thirty- or even forty-something husband is still a little boy inside who used to say to his mom, 'Watch me! Watch me!' They never completely get over that."

Speaking softly is avoiding any speech that would make life bitter for your spouse. It's buffering hard truth with endearments like "babe." It's laying the foundation of positive talk to support the occasional corrective talk.

You cannot build an intimate marriage with harsh words and verbal assaults. That's like trying to plant seeds on concrete. When you think cherish, think "soft." Think, "How can I be a healing presence in my spouse's life?"

Affirm the Gospel

One of the best ways to cherish your spouse with words is by affirming the gospel—the essential message of Christianity—and regularly planting its truth in your lover's heart and mind. Sometimes we have to remind our spouses of the gospel—total and complete acceptance before God because of the finished work of Jesus Christ on the cross—because some of them brush the teeth of their own worst enemy every day. They are so hard on themselves that they've essentially become an enemy to their own happiness. With earnest hearts, the standard they've set for themselves and their refusal to embrace grace are such that no one criticizes them more than they do.

We need to be a dissenting, steady, and persistent voice counterbalancing all the negative, guilt-ridden stuff with God's forgiveness, pardon, affirmation, acceptance, and lavishly undeserved love.

If you grew up thinking of God as a harsh taskmaster; if you're not familiar with what "speaking the gospel" to your spouse means, consider the following biblical examples.

Consider, for instance, how God viewed Rahab. She was a prostitute and a liar, and her own countrymen could have called her a traitor. Why, for instance, do you think she was so quickly able to hide Israel's spies from her own people? A prostitute back then had to be very adept at hiding men when their wives or male relatives came looking for them. It's not a coincidence that she immediately knew where two men could quickly and effectively hide. She had experience in the worst sort of way, yet God used that experience in the best kind of way—accomplishing his plan for the Israelites. And so God commends Rahab as a "woman of faith" who gave a hospitable welcome to Israel's spies (Hebrews 11:31). *She is commended for hiding two men, not condemned for sleeping with hundreds.*

Also consider Noah. He once drank so much he passed out and then cursed one of his sons out of his own embarrassment. Yet God declared him to be an "heir of the righteousness that is in keeping with faith" (Hebrews 11:7).

And what about Sarah? Sarah laughed—she *laughed*—at the angel of God who told her she would conceive a child in her old age. Did God remember her laugh? On the contrary, "And by faith even Sarah, who was past childbearing age, was enabled to bear children because she considered him faithful who had made the promise" (Hebrews 11:11). Sarah considered him faithful? Funny, *I* don't remember reading that it went down like that.

But God does.

We could also remember Job, who, let's be honest (just read his own words), murmured against God, cursed the day he was born, certainly complained, and seemed very impatient in the face of his maladies, yet how does God's Word describe him? "You have heard of Job's perseverance" (James 5:11).

The perseverance of Job. That's how God remembers him.

If you're in Christ and if your spouse is in Christ, God doesn't see your worst or even pettiest sins. He sees Christ in you. Consequently, he sees the faith you've exercised. He sees the good works you've done. He sees the glory he put in you by his Holy Spirit.

I want you and your spouse to walk in the joy of forgiveness and grace, your rightful excitement that, as a child of God forgiven by Christ and empowered by the Holy Spirit, everything bad you've done is forgotten—gone!—and everything good is celebrated and remembered.

Satan doesn't just *tempt* your spouse; he tries to *discourage* your spouse, and the gospel is the best remedy to build up your spouse in the face of his or her daily battle with sin. Speak words of God's acceptance and affirmation to each other. On a date night, read Romans 3:21–26 together, talking about how this truth impacts your marriage and parenting:

> But now apart from the law the righteousness of God has been made known, to which the Law and the Prophets testify. This righteousness is given through faith in Jesus Christ to all who believe. There is no difference between Jew and Gentile, for all have sinned and fall short of the glory of God, and all are justified freely by his grace through the redemption that came by Christ Jesus. God presented Christ as a sacrifice of atonement, through the shedding of his blood—to be received by faith. He did this to demonstrate his righteousness, because in his forbearance he had left the sins committed beforehand unpunished—he did it to demonstrate his righteousness in the present time, so as to be just and the one who justifies those who have faith in Jesus.

On another night, read all of Romans 5—too long to copy here—a great thing to do on a date. And always be ready to speak Romans 8:1–4 whenever you hear your spouse launch into self-despising talk.

> Therefore, there is now no condemnation for those who are in Christ Jesus, because through Christ Jesus the law of the Spirit who gives life has set you free from the law of sin and

death. For what the law was powerless to do because it was weakened by the flesh, God did by sending his own Son in the likeness of sinful flesh to be a sin offering. And so he condemned sin in the flesh, in order that the righteous requirement of the law might be fully met in us, who do not live according to the flesh but according to the Spirit.

On vacation, take out your Bible and discuss Ephesians 1:3–8, 13–14:

> Praise be to the God and Father of our Lord Jesus Christ, who has blessed us in the heavenly realms with every spiritual blessing in Christ. For he chose us in him before the creation of the world to be holy and blameless in his sight. In love he predestined us for adoption to sonship through Jesus Christ, in accordance with his pleasure and will—to the praise of his glorious grace, which he has freely given us in the One he loves. In him we have redemption through his blood, the forgiveness of sins, in accordance with the riches of God's grace that he lavished on us . . .

> And you also were included in Christ when you heard the message of truth, the gospel of your salvation. When you believed, you were marked in him with a seal, the promised Holy Spirit, who is a deposit guaranteeing our inheritance until the redemption of those who are God's possession—to the praise of his glory.

These truths never get old. We need to be reminded of them every day. The best gift we can give our spouses and children is the assurance of the gospel.

Please don't pass over that last sentence: more precious than a pure gold necklace, more lovely than diamond earrings, more beautiful than two dozen roses, and more refreshing to a man than an ice-cold tea or beer (whatever his preference) on a hot summer day is to proclaim the truth, glory, and pardon of God's gospel message to your spouse.

Here's a side benefit: a joyful person walking in grace and hope can cherish much more than one who is tangled up in the guilt that Christ died to remove. Our guilt serves no one. In Christ, our self-condemnation offends God; it doesn't please him. To walk in condemnation is to call God a liar and Christ's work insufficient. One of the worst sins you can commit as a Christian is to define yourself by your sin. In the same way, one of the worst sins you can commit against your spouse is to always define them by their sin. Biblical marriage is about defining each other as Christ defines us—saved sons and daughters who are growing more magnificent every day as they are eventually made perfect by Christ himself at the end.

When our guilt has been duly dealt with, definitively and powerfully, and when our acceptance has been declared by an authority that far exceeds our own, then finally we can embrace something far superior to "you're special." We can embrace "you're forgiven, adopted, and secure. You're *cherished* by the God of the universe—the King of kings and the Lord of lords."

Remind your spouse of this precious truth. In the dark days and cold nights, don't let them forget the spiritual riches they enjoy. These are the most precious words you could ever utter.

CHERISHING CHERISH

- To have a cherishing marriage, we need to be intentional about the way we speak to each other— not just the content, but the tone as well.

- To cherish our spouses with words requires maintaining our curiosity. We should ask them for more information, not ignore what they're saying or try to cut them off.

- When we correct our spouses, we need to find a way to still cherish them in the midst of the correction. We may have to ask them how best to do this.

- Cherishing words are specific, deliberate, and soft.

- One of the best ways to verbally cherish our spouses is to speak the gospel to them, regularly reminding them of God's acceptance and affirmation.

QUESTIONS FOR DISCUSSION AND REFLECTION

1. Try to recall your last five or six marital conversations—in person or on the phone. Did your tone cherish or alienate your spouse? After thinking about it, ask for your spouse's recollection.

2. When is the last time you asked your spouse for more information when they started sharing something important to them?

3. Is there any area in your marriage where you need to learn how to say, "This way, hon"? Ask your spouse if they think you're regularly having conversations that seem to create distance between the two of you, and discuss how you can learn to communicate in a way that creates feelings of being cherished.

4. Think of three specific things you cherish about your spouse. Tell them what they are! If you're in a group setting, let others hear you speak of how excellent and wonderful your spouse truly is.

5. Find a few creative ways to remind your spouse, "Hey, God is crazy about you. And you know, don't you, that your heavenly Father delights in you?"

6. On a future date night or morning together, read Romans 3:21-26; on another night, read all of Romans 5. Then consider using Romans 8:1-4 and Ephesians 1:3-14. Try to intentionally use Scripture to fuel your conversations.

CHAPTER 9

Cherish Your Unique Spouse

Cherishing is about treating our spouses as unique individuals

Following one of Texas's famous rainstorms, Lisa and I pulled into a rest home parking lot, each of us driving our own car. We had to go to different places following our visit with our ninety-eight-year-old friend.

The parking lot was under water at the outer edges, but all the other spaces were taken, so that's where Lisa parked. When we came out after our visit, one of the workers had wheeled an elderly person toward the curb. She was near where Lisa parked, which was surrounded by water. I took Lisa's keys, jumped in the car, and slowly backed it out so Lisa didn't have to trek through the puddle and make it through a tight spot, with other cars and a wheelchair and oxygen stand blocking the way.

This was expected in our marriage. When I held out my hand, Lisa instinctively handed over her keys without asking what I was doing. We didn't even talk about it. That's just what we do. In a situation like that, I'm going to move the car because it makes Lisa feel cared for and loved. But in other marriages, what I had done might be treated with resentment. I can imagine NASCAR driver Danica Patrick's future husband offering to back her car out of a tight spot and Danica being offended and saying, "Not a chance. And by the way, I'll race you home!"

I've never met your spouse, but I know your spouse is very different from mine. Every spouse is.

While reading a wonderful book on marriage, I came across spectacular advice that would be harmful in one of the marriages I've worked with. This writer suggested, "I learned that the most romantic gesture I can offer Christi is simply asking about her day, how she's feeling, and what's going on in her heart and mind."

I think this author is exactly right—for the vast majority of marriages. But I was invited into the lives of a couple heavily involved in ministry, and they don't fit the stereotype for husbands and wives. The husband's earnest desire for deep relating actually created a challenge in his marriage rather than being a strength.

Usually—i.e., stereotypically—the wife wants the husband to be more relationally "evolved." This man was that—he loved pressing toward greater relational intimacy and deeper conversation. Yet for a variety of reasons, his wife felt uncomfortable with "relational discussions." She didn't like exploring her feelings and wasn't all that in touch with them, and when her husband tried to have these discussions, she felt insecure. Her family of origin never talked that way. As the wife, she knew she was supposed to be "better" at it than her husband, which just creates shame, so what this author is suggesting, while helpful to the vast majority of husbands, would in this woman's marriage be seen as a *threat*, not as an act of love.

Seriously.

If this husband asked his wife, "How are you feeling? What's going on in your heart and mind?" I can tell you right now the expression she'd get on her face and how she'd want to hide but know she shouldn't, which would make her feel ashamed, which would make her a little angry (justifiably so, perhaps) that her husband was putting her in this situation when he knew better, which would make her defensive, which would end in a predictable pattern that *no one* would describe as "romantic."

Still, it's spectacular advice—for *most* couples, just not for *this* couple.

Cherishing each other requires dealing with a real, particular spouse and is fueled by the spouse's uniqueness. If two-carat diamonds were as common as sand on a seashore, none of them would be cherished. But the fact that something is different makes it precious. That's why we cherish it—it's one of a kind. Your spouse is unique, special—and for them to feel cherished, they need to be *treated as such*.

When you read books and blogs by marriage authors like me, never forget that what matters most is *your* marriage and *your* spouse. When it comes to marital issues like intimate relating—including sexuality, but also conversation, certain aspects of various roles, and preferred activities—these are so personal and so often deeply stamped into our souls long before we become husband and wife that we've got to start building our marriages on a "blank slate."

If you cherish what you think your wife *should* be instead of what she really is, you'll actually do harm to the relationship. If you cherish your husband the way most husbands would like to be cherished, you're going to run into a wall if your husband isn't a "typical" husband.

Your husband is who he is; your wife is who she is. Find out who that person is, and cherish that person as they desire to be cherished.

A Unique Bed

A man entered marriage with quite a bit of prior sexual experience—but not with his wife. After encountering Jesus, he and his future wife decided to follow a different plan for their relationship, so they waited until the wedding night before they slept together. They then faced years of frustration because the wife simply did not enjoy what was happening in the bedroom. Her husband thought it was all her fault, since he had pleased "plenty of women" before they got married. It got so bad they finally sought out a counselor. The husband thought something was "wrong" with his wife. When she protested that she didn't enjoy what he was doing, he blurted out, "But women *like* that!"

The counselor wisely responded, "Not *this* woman, and she's the only one who matters."

The husband's previous sexual experience had actually made cherishing one woman more difficult for him. He made assumptions about women in general that blinded him to the reality of his wife in particular. *Cherishing is all about the particular.* You learn how to cherish your spouse by studying them, listening to them, and finding out who they are, what motivates them, what pleases them, what hurts them, what scares them, what fulfills them, and what makes them laugh.

A cherishing marriage is built on intimate understanding, not stereotypical assumptions. Don't apply spectacular advice that is true in 90 percent of marriages if it's not true in yours—because if it's not true in yours, it's spectacularly *bad* advice.

Booooo!

Ann Wilson married a famous man. Her husband, Dave, was a College Hall of Fame quarterback who was the number one pick, selected by the New Orleans Saints, in the 1981 supplemental National Football League draft.

You may remember that I talked in a previous chapter about how so many spouses feel discouraged and beat-up when they enter marriage, giving voice to the vast legions of us who never felt like we truly measured up.

That's not Dave. His family of origin was such that Dave became the apple of his mom's eye and the focus of her attention, and he excelled in high school. Not only was he a quarterback, but in basketball he was the point guard and in baseball he played shortstop—all the glamorous positions. Even more, he was a lead singer and guitar player in a rock band, not to mention homecoming king and the most sought-after date on campus.

Today he's lead pastor at Kensington Community Church, a national multicampus church that welcomes fourteen thousand attenders every weekend. Plus, he's one of the most likeable guys I've ever met. When a guy is that successful, the dark side of you kind of wants to dislike him, but there's something about Dave that is so inviting and infectious that you'd have to have an inordinately self-absorbed and insecure soul to not enjoy being around him. If somebody's going to succeed at that level, he's the best kind of guy to do it.

When Dave got married, he was used to being cheered—by his mom, by coaches and teammates, by cheerleaders, by people at his church. Whether it was in sports, music, or even worship, he was "the man." When Ann agreed to marry him, it was yet another "accomplishment" for Dave. A beautiful, vivacious, and spiritually alive woman agreed to spend her life with him; Dave felt like it may have been his best "win" yet (but he didn't personally look at it that crassly).

Here's the challenge for Ann—marry a superstar husband, and even a superstar begins to appear "normal" after a while. Ann looked at all that Dave brought to the relationship and thought, *That's what men are supposed to do and supposed to be.* But very few men are that accomplished, confident, successful, and financially well-off.

It was during a joint speaking event that Ann finally understood something that had been hurting Dave for a long time. She asked him to explain something to the wives, and Dave got a spontaneous picture in his mind.

"Sometimes," he said, "it feels like I've been cheered my whole life—by my mom, coaches, fellow students, cheerleaders, people who come to church, people who used to listen to my music—but then I'd come home and I'd hear (Dave paused here, cupped his hands around his mouth like an unruly fan does during a football game, and shouted) 'Booo, boooo, boooo!'"

Dave didn't understand how he could please so many people and yet so deeply disappoint one wife. Ann was shocked when she heard this illustration; she felt awful. She realized she had let Dave set the bar of expectations so high that she didn't fully appreciate the fact that he was rather special. To cherish Dave, she had to figure out how to affirm a highly successful man.

Dave will tell you that from that moment on, everything changed in their marriage. The way Ann talked to him, the words she chose, the things she noticed and pointed out. While some women have to build up beaten-down husbands, Ann, in one sense had to compete with an affirming world that had already built up her husband.

Dave told me that since that day, Ann goes out of her way to appreciate him. "Not a week goes by without Ann telling me I'm a good provider or thanking me for leading the family spiritually and making my relationship with Jesus a priority."

Ann adds, "The reason I didn't do that before is I thought that's what a man is *supposed* to do, so why should I thank him for it or point it out? But then I realized not all men are like that. Dave really is special."

With several married sons, Ann has seen firsthand "how crazy it is—the power a woman has over her husband."

You could be married to the most successful woman or man alive, but if they hear you yelling "booo!" there will still be an ache in their souls.

What's your spouse's unique past? Are you competing with their successes, encouraging them through their past failures, helping them to grow into their accomplishments, or trying to assure them their worth is not tied to what they do? These are all competing goals; your spouse has a unique history, so cherish your spouse by treating them according to their reality: *They are living a life that has never been lived before.* They have a personality that has never existed before. They have a unique blend of strengths and weaknesses, temptations and gifts, as well as a once-in-the-universe calling.

Your role is to help them complete their one-of-a-kind story.

Recognize You Don't Know How to Cherish Your Spouse

Since your spouse is special, a new attitude of cherishing her or him must be based on humble learning and empathetic study, not on trying to "guess and impress." Set aside time to ask your spouse, "What makes you feel cherished? Tell me the top three times you've felt cherished by me. Have there been any times when you sensed I was trying to cherish you, but I made some faulty assumptions?"

When we first got married, Lisa started a journal called "Gary." She wrote down things she noticed about me—what I liked, what irritated me, little things I mentioned. She was trying to study me in a way similar to taking notes at a college lecture. I don't know how many entries she put into it or if the journal is still active, but it reveals the depth of her cherishing heart that she felt it necessary to study me.

Be humble here. No matter how high your relational EQ is, you can't possibly know how to cherish your spouse without him or her helping you, because every soul is a unique country that—sadly—is often left unexplored. Many husbands and wives divorce spouses they don't actually know. They think they do, but they've never truly taken the time to admit they don't know how to cherish their spouse. And so they tried to cherish out of their own understanding, failed miserably, and then blamed their spouse for not feeling cherished: "He [she] just can't be pleased."

If you start out with the assumption that you don't know how to cherish your spouse, you'll go much further in eventually excelling in cherishing him or her. Plus, pursuing your spouse in this way adds interest to the marriage. It assaults boredom.

Even after thirty-one years of marriage, I know there is much for me to find out about Lisa. Why? Because now she's a mother-in-law. That changes a woman. Now she's an empty nester. That changes a woman too. As life changes, so my wife changes. There is always a new person to get to know, a new person to learn how to cherish.

Post Pictures

A simple practical tool I use to cultivate cherishing my unique wife is to keep a favorite photograph of Lisa in my walk-in closet. I get dressed there every morning, and I see a picture of Lisa that, for whatever reason, fills me with delight for her. It captures her light, her beauty, her personality; it reminds me of how I cherish her.

So I want to look at it as I begin each day.

Every married person would do well to have a favorite picture—the kind that makes your heart melt. It doesn't matter if the picture is twenty years old. All that matters is that it elicits feelings of cherishing your spouse.

Pornography is based on and fed by always needing to see something *new*. It works neurologically to create an obsessive demand for more of something you've never seen before. The promise of something new is what gets you excited and interested, which means, by definition, that you can never be fully satisfied.

That's the opposite of cherish. Pornography works off volume, not individuality; it works off the novel, not the known. Learning to cherish a solo picture of a unique mate shapes our hearts and minds to cherish a particular individual above all others. It astonishes me to see how a favorite picture of my wife never gets old, never gets stale, never makes me want to click to see what's next. Perhaps because it's connected to a real person and a real relationship. I'm not a neuroscientist or psychologist, so what do I know? Just that a slightly flirtatious picture of my wife will be immensely more satisfying and enduring than anything much more explicit with a stranger.

Dig out a couple of old photos or post one on the wallpaper of your computer or your cell phone. If your spouse doesn't have a photo, for your next anniversary or Valentine's Day present, make one.

Revisit Misunderstandings

Bring to mind a lingering issue in your marriage that has resulted in long-term frustration. Have you been making assumptions about how your spouse *should* feel, *should* behave, *should* function, according to popular stereotype? You'll begin to cherish your spouse when you treat them like the unique individual they are.

For some of you (though, again, not all!), the best thing you can do is start over and assume your husband or wife isn't like most men or women. Get to know them all over again, listen to what really affirms or scares or frustrates them, and start relating to that person, the one you're married to. In the end, that's the only person who matters. Maybe some of you could even start a spouse journal, like my wife did—taking notes and trying to figure out her husband.

Megan Cox, a friend of mine, felt her heart melt when her husband, David, told her early on in their marriage, "I don't care

what other women like, Megan. I only care about what *you* like."
In Megan's words, "This opened my eyes to how well he loves
me. He embraced *me*, and I felt deeply cherished for the first
time in my life."

Men, it should be easy to see how this makes a wife feel
cherished. It tells her first that in one sense, she is the only
woman who matters to us—our Eve, the only woman in the
world. As Solomon wrote, "My dove, my perfect one, is the only
one" (Song of Songs 6:9 ESV).

And second, treating your wife this way tells her you love
her individuality—you love what makes her different and
unique. You love what makes her *her*. She doesn't have to look
like a swimsuit model or have the energy of a presidential can-
didate, the business savvy of Oprah, or the intellect of a college
professor.

She just has to be herself.

CHERISHING CHERISH

- Your spouse is a unique individual. Don't treat him or
  her like a stereotype.

- Good advice for other couples may be bad advice for
  you.

- The way our spouses relate and process emotions,
  fears, and dreams shouldn't be judged; it just has to
  be understood. This isn't to say there aren't healthy
  and unhealthy ways of relating, but learning to
  cherish our spouses must begin with understanding
  and empathizing with who they truly are.

- In any area of marriage, if you treat your spouse according to a stereotype or in a way that worked with previous boyfriends or girlfriends but doesn't work with your spouse, that doesn't mean there's something wrong with your spouse. It just means you need to relearn how to relate to the particular woman or man you married.

- Every spouse enters marriage with a unique story; cherishing your spouse means you have to learn and understand their story.

- To fully cherish your spouse, you have to humbly admit you don't yet know all you need to know about how to cherish them.

- Favorite photographs can sustain our affection and train our hearts to keep our focus on our unique and special spouse.

QUESTIONS FOR DISCUSSION AND REFLECTION

1. How are you different from most men (if you're a man) or women (if you're a woman)? Do you think your spouse is aware of this?

2. How does your spouse differ from "normal" people of their gender? How long did it take you to understand this?

3. So far, Gary has talked about spouses who entered marriage feeling beat-up emotionally, and in this

chapter he introduces us to one who was rather famous and confident. What are some other backgrounds and histories that can shape a spouse?

4. How can understanding the uniqueness of your spouse help you to cherish them even more rather than judging them?

5. Ask your spouse to tell you one thing about them that you don't yet know—something that makes them feel special, affirmed, cherished. Then ask them if there's something you do that makes them feel less than special, affirmed, or cherished.

6. Choose a favorite photograph and post it in a prominent place.

7. Given all you know and have learned, write out a prescription for how best to cherish your particular spouse.

CHAPTER 10

This Is How Your Spouse Stumbles

Cherishing means being patient with your spouse's sins

M ost iPhone owners love them, but after a year, the problem with a smartphone is that the battery gets weaker and weaker. It is glorious in the first six months when you plug in your phone at night and don't even think about power levels until the next evening. But at about nine months, you start to get nervous in midafternoon and make sure you recharge it so it can make it through the rest of the day.

After a year, you're plugging in your phone at lunchtime and then an hour before you leave the office, because the battery is getting weaker and weaker. At the end, you just leave it plugged in every chance you get.

This process, sadly, is never reversed. Once the battery starts draining, it just keeps draining faster and faster until you finally reach the typical two-year deadline to get a brand-new phone.

The same principle applies in many marriages. The passion

is so intense when the relationship is new that it seems to charge itself, even when you're apart. It doesn't need special care. It doesn't need to be plugged in. It seems to supply its own passion. Cherish seems to generate itself, a "perpetual emotion" machine. But sooner rather than later, the passion begins to drain. Thus begins the downward slide that, sadly, is sometimes never reversed until the couple gives up, trades each other in, and gets a new partner to cherish.

The reason our relationships tend to drain, spiritually speaking, is because of our fallen nature—the little unkindnesses, our natural selfishness, our impatience, low-grade—or even full-blown—addictions, things we call sins. These small, daily spiritual assaults slowly harden the soft heart of cherishing our spouses. If you believe the Bible, every person fails in many ways and on many occasions, which means every married person who is bent on cherishing their spouse has to confront a major spiritual truth: "we all stumble in many ways" (James 3:2).

If we allow our spouses' stumbling to assault how much we cherish them, no one can sustain a cherishing attitude.

Even those of us who have unusually easy spouses to cherish can fall prey to this. On one occasion, one of Lisa's most common issues cropped up, and I found myself momentarily feeling sorry for myself (showing my stupidity)—until God stopped my thinking with the force of a referee blowing a whistle in my face:

"This is how your spouse stumbles."

Lisa stumbles far less than the average spouse—of that I'm certain—and I've taught and written about James 3:2 ("we all stumble in many ways") thousands of times. But two decades into marriage ministry and three decades into marriage,

I still find myself momentarily resentful of the fact that I don't have a 100-percent-perfect wife—even though her excellence exceeds mine.

Some of you exhaust your friends and even try God's patience by recounting the same thing over and over: "why must my spouse stumble like this?" Your friends would do well to say—and if you would listen, you would likely hear God say—"if he [she] didn't stumble like this, then they would be stumbling like *that*."

If you want to build a marriage in which you keep cherishing each other, you have to get over the hurdle of expecting your spouse to be perfect. No one would suggest, intellectually, that we expect our spouses to be perfect; we all would say, "Of course my spouse stumbles," but in our hearts, don't we often resent the *particular* way our spouses stumble, at the very least telling ourselves, "Wouldn't it be much better if he [she] stumbled in a different way?"

Don't we think, *I could cherish them if only they wouldn't do x, y, or z?*

To keep cherishing each other, it follows that we must be good forgivers, people who are eager to show mercy as we have been shown mercy. The goal of a cherishing marriage is to know each other so well that we know the dark corners and the weak links of each other's personalities and yet still cherish, respect, adore, and move toward each other.

The next time you find yourself complaining about your spouse, just remember these six words—"this is how your spouse stumbles"—and *get over it*. (Of course, I'm not talking about abuse or overtly destructive behavior.) Marriage is the art of learning how your spouse stumbles and cherishing them through it. Yes, love can mean helping them deal with their issues—or even overcome certain issues—but never, ever, get to the point that you expect your spouse to never stumble. Otherwise, you won't cherish them; you'll resent them.

The Other Side of Holiness

Your ability to cherish your spouse when they stumble is, in fact, a direct barometer of your spiritual maturity. If you look at the Bible's teaching, half of holiness centers around being patient with other people's sins, as much as it involves dealing with—or avoiding—our own sins.

Read these calls to holiness slowly, opening your mind to a new perspective:

- "Live a life worthy of the calling you have received. Be completely humble and gentle; be patient, bearing with one another in love. Make every effort to keep the unity of the Spirit through the bond of peace" (Ephesians 4:1–3).
- "Be patient with everyone" (1 Thessalonians 5:14).
- "As God's chosen people, holy and dearly loved, clothe yourselves with compassion, kindness, humility, gentleness and patience. Bear with each other and forgive one another" (Colossians 3:12–13).

These passages tie holiness almost exclusively to how we treat others who are messing up or in need: we respond with compassion, kindness, humility (not thinking we're better), gentleness, and patience, bearing (i.e., putting up!) with each other and forgiving one another. A holy person isn't known by what he or she does or doesn't watch, by avoiding a few forbidden words, or by attending a frequent number of religious meetings, but by how he or she treats fellow sinners. *Our experiential holiness is defined in large part by our ability to gracefully bear the lack of holiness in others.*

You know you are a spiritually strong person when you can live joyfully and gracefully around spiritually weak people.

The Bible never pretends Christian communities or marriages are successful because the members are close to perfect. No, the relationships become successful only when we apply grace to each other's imperfections. Consider how nice it would be to live out the truth of Ephesians 4:1–3, which lays out the biblical foundation for cherishing each other:

- *Humility.* You never look at yourself as better than your spouse. You don't look down on your spouse.
- *Gentleness.* You don't respond harshly to your spouse's sin. You watch your tone, your attitude, your touch. You treat your spouse like they can be hurt easily, so you're gentle and thoughtful in the face of their imperfections.
- *Patience.* You don't expect your spouse to be perfect. You don't lie in wait for them to mess up and then pounce when they do. You don't prepare a lecture ahead of time and then unleash it when your spouse inevitably stumbles. Instead, you take a deep breath, speak with an understanding tone, remember where you also fall short, and wait for them to grow.
- *Forbearance*—able to deal with a difficult person without becoming angry. You master the art of dealing with the worst parts of your spouse's personality in the best sort of way. You figure out how not to allow their sin to

elicit the worst in you, but rather how to call out God's Spirit in you so you can respond in the best sort of way. You don't impose time limits for change, and you never remind your spouse of past failings. You let go of your resentment and frustration.

There's another way of looking at this: if God's attitude toward you in your sin mirrored exactly your attitude toward your spouse in his or her sin, where would you be with God?

If you think you are a stronger, more mature Christian than your spouse, I know this: you compare yourself to your spouse instead of comparing yourself to Christ. Nowhere does the Bible urge you to compare yourself to your spouse.

Stop comparing your spiritual maturity with your spouse's; instead, start comparing your spiritual maturity with Ephesians 4:1–3. If you do that, you will change the climate of your marriage. Whenever your spouse stumbles, you will respond with gentleness, patience, kindness, humility, and long-suffering forgiveness; this response will allow you to keep cherishing a spouse who stumbles in many ways.

Recovery Involves Relapse

"Gary," the fortysomething wife said, "if a husband looks at porn, that's offensive, right—and it doesn't matter how long it's been, right? That doesn't make it okay."

Her emphasis told me what was going on. Her husband had "a past." After a long period in recovery, he'd had a relapse, and the two of them probably had a conversation that went something like this:

"I can't believe you did that again. You're so weak."

"Babe, I've tried really hard. It's been three months—"

"That doesn't matter! It's wrong, no matter how long it's been!"

What that wife said is technically true. If something is wrong, it doesn't matter if you do it every three months or every three days. It's still wrong.

Talking to my friends who have studied addiction, I've been astonished to learn that once an addictive pattern has been set, the neurological grooves are pretty much permanent. That's why alcoholics have to stay focused. If you get lackadaisical and the same old triggers show up—and you're not prepared—your brain is now predisposed to give in. The groove is set. You can have enjoyed freedom for ten years, but you're still more vulnerable than someone who doesn't have an addicted neurological pattern.

As experts put it, recovery often involves relapse. In fact, one of the leading books on one particular type of addiction views recovery as a *five-year process*. If a spouse doesn't understand this, instead of celebrating that her husband has triumphed over something that used to trip him up almost daily, she ends up making light of his ninety days of freedom—not insignificant—and using his episode of failure as just another point of attack. No, she can't (and she shouldn't) "celebrate" his fall, but which of these responses is most likely to lead to redemptive change?

- "Babe, I'm sorry. You've done so well, and I'm proud at how hard you have worked and how long you've had success. Let's talk about what happened this time."
- "Again? After you promised me you wouldn't? I knew I'd never be able to trust you!"

It's not easy to cherish a person who fails, but cherish is one of the most effective paths to help someone fail *less*. That's the challenge. Now, I'm not suggesting cherish is appropriate for an addict in denial who isn't in recovery and who isn't making the effort, but if someone is struggling, receiving help, and walking in grace and repentance, then being cherished will strengthen them and improve the odds that they will walk even longer in victory and ultimately find more freedom.

But not perfectly. Maybe *never* perfectly.

It sounds backward, but the more we cherish an imperfect spouse walking in progressive sanctification, the less imperfect he or she will likely become.* The less we cherish an imperfect spouse, the less impact we'll have on their eventual change. No spouse should ever feel alone on their journey toward transformation.

Real spouses get sick. They get cranky. They have bad days. If this resets how much we cherish and value them, we will lose our hearts for them. You didn't marry a goddess with supernatural powers over human limitations. You didn't marry a man with the wisdom of Solomon, the strength of Hercules, and the kindness of Christ; you married a man or woman whose body can break down, who is affected by stress, who cries when she is hurt, who usually complains when he gets sick, and who stumbles in many ways.

Accept his or her humanity. Remind yourself: this is how my spouse stumbles.

---

* "Progressive sanctification" is the phrase theologians use to describe how we grow in holiness day by day. Experiential holiness isn't achieved in a single prayer; it's developed over time. In contrast, positional holiness, which describes how God views us in light of Christ's sacrifice on our behalf, is instantaneous and doesn't change.

Here's the delightful irony: if you truly want a better spouse, learn to cherish the imperfect spouse you already have—and they're likely to become that better spouse.

Lost Keys

Let me give just one example of a situation that turned out well, a time when I learned to protect an attitude of cherishing my wife even in a moment of frustration.

One morning, I didn't wake up until 5:00 a.m.—a rarity for me. That also meant I was in danger of facing very heavy traffic traveling in from the Houston suburb where I used to live.

I rushed through my shower-and-shave routine and then couldn't find my keys anywhere. I double- and then triple-checked every possible spot, realizing that every minute at home meant another two or three minutes on the road. I could *feel* the traffic backing up on I-10.

After going through our bedroom with my cellphone flashlight for the third time, Lisa stirred.

"What's the matter?" she asked.

"I can't find my car keys anywhere."

"Oh, I'm so sorry! They're in my purse. I had to drive your car last night." (She hadn't been able to find her keys the night before, so she had taken my car.)

She got out of bed, and we both began searching for her purse. Lisa had gotten home late and was tired, and it takes Lisa's brain a while to wake up, so even finding her *purse* took some time!

Finally we found the purse—and thus the keys.

"I'm so sorry," Lisa said over and over. She knew the traffic patterns. She knew how frustrating it is for me to not get an early start.

I tenderly kissed her, put my voice on soft mode, and said, "Don't worry about it, honey."

I knew Lisa wasn't trying to make life difficult for me. Yelling at her or trying to explain my exasperation would have been useless. She knew I was frustrated, and she knew the consequences of what had happened—and none of it was intentional on her end. This is one of the things in marriage that, in my view, you just have to let go. What would have been served by hashing it out, being angry, yelling, or letting her know how frustrated I was?

Leaving the house well past 6:00 a.m. and facing an hour commute, I stopped at a Starbucks, got some tea, and told myself I was going to settle in and listen to the podcast I had downloaded. I wasn't going to fret. I wasn't going to have an imaginary conflict-resolution conversation with Lisa. I was going to relax and prepare for the day.

If I had yelled at Lisa and stomped out of the house, I would have spent the next several hours in a foul mood—unable to relax, enjoy my tea, or focus on my work. Choosing the right words and attitudes with which to cherish my wife probably blessed me more than it blessed her.

These common life events reset the climate in every marriage. If you know in your mind that your spouse stumbles, what is served by making them pay for it? Does it make them stumble less? Does it make you happier? Does it remove a single consequence from what happened—or does it simply add to your frustration and grief?

Lisa called a few hours later to apologize. We were in a busy time; she was running ragged throughout the day, and I told her that forgetting to put my keys back where I usually keep them was understandable. Stuff like that just happens.

When such life frustrations arrive, remember that the art of cherishing your mate is reminding yourself—not with bitterness, but with spiritual understanding—*this is how your spouse stumbles*. As Solomon once wrote, "Those with good sense are slow to anger, and it is their glory to overlook an offense" (Proverbs 19:11 NRSV).

Look at the Presence behind the Problem

I have two talk radio programs I like to download and listen to on a regular basis. I know it must be tedious at times for Lisa to overhear them while I'm showering or driving (especially when I'm listening to the sports one), so I asked her one morning, "Are you okay with this? I don't want to be doing something so frequently that it annoys you."

"Of course it's fine," Lisa said. "Hearing it means you're home."

Lisa wouldn't choose these programs on her own, but she recognizes that their sounds signify her husband's presence, so she welcomes them.

Guys, your wives might make you late—but that means they're alive and a part of your lives. Women, your husbands might leave the toilet seat up, but that means they woke up in the same house you slept in.

When you truly cherish someone, you look at the *presence* behind the *problem*. If you've accepted that every spouse stumbles in many ways, then you know it's not possible to have the positive presence of a spouse without a corresponding frustration or disappointment. So you look at the frustration as a marker of blessing: this is how the spouse you cherish occasionally stumbles. Since what you cherish brings you pleasure, the occasional problem is a price you're willing to pay to be with the one you cherish.

Give Your Spouse the Benefit of the Doubt

Brian and Dyanna married young, and partly because they had a Sunday school teacher tell them they should pray seriously about whether birth control was biblical, Dyanna found herself pregnant at twenty-one.

Dyanna was a young bride with a growing belly as she and Brian walked through a mall on a cheap date. At this point, Dyanna was more than eight months pregnant. A beautiful young blonde woman, lithe and athletic, walked by, and Brian said, "Dang, I forgot how pretty you are when you're not pregnant."

"Yes, he said it!" Dyanna remembers. "And yes, he meant it."

Dyanna started sobbing uncontrollably, but Brian had no idea why.

Here's the graciousness of Dyanna's character, which helps to explain why they have been happily married for twenty-five years: "Brian's heart had no malice. He actually believed he was paying me a compliment. He was, in fact, completely caught off guard when I began to sob uncontrollably. He had no idea what was wrong.

"I cherished Brian by knowing his character, which allowed me to recover quickly and laugh about this for years to come. Brian thought he was cherishing me by comparing me to a beautiful girl who reminded him of me eight months earlier. His words got all mixed-up and came out wrong.

"A young bride may not have the capacity to understand the thoughts of a young husband; everything is so new. But she can cherish him by giving him the benefit of the doubt. Would Brian ever have said something like that to be intentionally cruel and hurtful? Not a chance. He was trying to compliment me. It took me a few minutes to realize that, but now this is a fun memory, not a bitter one."

When someone pledges to be your spouse, that commitment alone should earn him or her the benefit of the doubt. Even when things may not look the best, seek understanding before you even think about censure. Cherishing our spouses doesn't mean living in Fantasyland, but it does mean giving our spouses the benefit of the doubt instead of jumping immediately to accusation. Showing initial support is a way to honor and cherish your spouse until you figure out what actually happened.

When you must confront your spouse, begin with an open-ended question; don't prepare a speech. "Tell me what happened from your perspective" is a much better opening than "how could you do such a thing?" The "ask first" approach launches a potentially redemptive conversation rather than a fight.

Having a fantasy conversation in advance of talking to your spouse doesn't help either. It assumes all that's needed is for your spouse to hear what you think, not that you need to hear what he or she was thinking.

I can't put this forcefully enough: *start these conversations with questions that seek understanding, not with accusations that seek submission.* The former breeds cherishing; the latter feeds emotional distance.

This is even true, spouses, when you are married to someone who is recovering. It's possible and perhaps even natural that an addict is immediately accused when something happens and it seems on the surface that a previous pattern is repeating itself. Force yourself to pause long enough to silently pray. If your spouse is repenting and is being falsely accused, your belief in them could be so healing, *even a life-defining moment.* You have no idea what it means when everyone is doubting you but your spouse is standing behind you. Enabling denial is, of course, wrong and unhelpful. But showing initial support isn't enabling and isn't denial. It's simply wanting to hear your spouse's side before you jump to any conclusion. Every spouse deserves that.

A short summary, then: when your spouse stumbles, a helpful cool-down thought is the simple "this is how my spouse stumbles." Our maturity in Christ is defined by how gracious we are with regard to how our spouse's stumbling inconveniences us. Cherishing means we don't allow our spouse's stumbling to create distance, but rather we intentionally craft a generous, gentle, and kind response that builds appreciation and intimacy. This is the only way we can keep our marriage's "cherishing batteries" charged in the face of the reality that we all stumble in many ways.

CHERISHING CHERISH

- We need to accept the fact that our spouses will stumble and stop resenting that they happen to stumble in any particular way.

- The goal of a cherishing marriage is to know the dark corners and the weak links of each other's personalities, yet still cherish, respect, adore, and move toward each other.

- Holiness, according to the Bible, is often best demonstrated by how patient we are with the lack of holiness in others.

- Cherish is a long-term strategy that encourages a stumbling spouse to stumble a little less.

- Brace yourself: recovery usually involves relapse.

- Look for the "presence behind the problem." Since no spouse is perfect, remind yourself that an occasional stumble is the price you pay to have another person in your life.

- Responding with gentleness to common marital moments—like a spouse misplacing your keys— can be the seedbed of a cherishing marriage. Ask yourself: is a confrontation really necessary, given that they didn't intend to cause me harm and already feel bad about what happened?

- Give your spouse the benefit of the doubt. Start potentially heated conversations with questions instead of accusations. Seek understanding, not an opportunity to give a lecture.

QUESTIONS FOR DISCUSSION AND REFLECTION

1. Think of two or three ways in which you stumble most frequently in your marriage. What does your spouse have to put up with?

2. Consider one or two areas where you know your spouse regularly stumbles. Is this something you need to accept, apply patience to, or directly confront? Try to consider, in the light of what we discussed in this chapter, the most appropriate response.

3. If holiness is defined as patiently enduring the sins and failings of others, what kind of "holiness grade" would you give yourself over the last week? The past year?

4. If recovery involves relapse, what appropriate accountability measures need to be considered so your patience doesn't become a matter of codependence—i.e., enabling an unhealthy pattern to continue?

5. What are some of the benefits of your spouse's presence that will help you endure some of the inevitable irritations of living with them?

6. Describe a recent marital spat that, in retrospect, should have been let go—i.e., looking back on it, instead of trying to "work it out," you now wish you would have just reminded yourself, "This is how my spouse stumbles" and moved on.

7. How important is it to you that your spouse gives you the benefit of the doubt? Do you feel you usually receive that? How often do you do this for your spouse?

CHAPTER 11

The Art of Cherishing Your Spouse

Crafting a cherishing mind-set

You can pay $25,000 for a watch that will never disappoint you. It will tell time with mathematical precision. If you look at it fifteen times a day, it will serve you each time—and never get tired doing so.

And it will never complain if you look at it a sixteenth time.

You can take it off in the evening and put it on in the morning, and that watch won't whine that it has been ignored all night long, that you are just using it. It won't ask you for a birthday or anniversary present; it won't make any demands on you. It will just tell you what you need to know, look attractive on your wrist, and exist solely to meet your specific needs.

But who wants to be married to a watch?

More people than you might think.

Husbands and wives often treat each other according to whatever roles they expect from each other. "Just do what you're supposed to do and try to look reasonably attractive while you're doing it, and everything will be fine."

The problem with this kind of thinking is that husbands and wives are souls who want to be married to someone who will cherish the whole person, not just a particular role a person may fulfill.

Because life is so busy and there are so many demands on us, we have to intentionally build a cherishing mind-set or risk valuing our spouses not for who they are but for what they do. Someone valued only for what they do feels like an employee, not a cherished spouse.

Neuroplasticity

Jesus said that Christian fruit comes from those who "hear the word, hold it fast in an honest and good heart, and bear fruit with *patient endurance*" (Luke 8:15 NRSV, italics added).

Jesus' words about bearing fruit with "patient endurance" (steadily, over the long haul) predate neurological science by almost two millennia, but since he designed the brain, it shouldn't surprise us that, scientifically speaking, he was thousands of years ahead of his time in understanding human nature. Neurologists (those who study the brain) now describe how our brains are literally and physiologically shaped by our experience over time. We fashion grooves in our brains that often direct our actions. Repeated actions impact our brain so powerfully that whatever that action is becomes our default mode of response.

This explains how you learn to play an instrument. At first, you have to think about where to put your fingers when you see an A# on the musical score. After a while, you see the A# and your fingers just go there. Even later, you don't even need the musical score; you just play the A# because you know—without even thinking about it—it's the note that comes next.

Think about a baseball player. When we were very young, if someone hit a ground ball at us, our natural instinct would be to move out of the way. With time and practice, our coaches taught us to move *toward* the ball in order to field it. What was once an unconscious decision to move away from the ball, after repetitive, intentional practice, becomes an unconscious reaction to move toward the ball. It would feel weird and unnatural for Bryce Harper to move away from a hard grounder or duck when a fly ball is coming his way.

That's neuroplasticity in action.

The same principle applies when learning to cherish, post-infatuation. We selfish, immature people have to think about *how* to cherish. We have to cultivate thankfulness and gratitude over bitterness and accusation. We have to be intentional rather than distracted. We have to remind ourselves to think about our spouses with delight. It's not *a* choice; it's a hundred choices, a thousand choices, and then a hundred thousand choices.

If we keep doing that, it's like we're planting a seed and then watering the ground, fertilizing around it, and weeding it. First we see the shoot, then the leaf, and finally the flower.

In other words, *we can grow cherish*. In the language of neurology, cherish is (forgive the 1970s pun) "groovy." We create the grooves by what we do, what we think about, and how we respond until it becomes our default mode of relating.

Learning to cherish is learning to shape the grooves in our brains. What, then, are some practical ways, in addition to what we've already discussed, to train our brains to choose cherish?

1. Use Your Mind to Charge Your Heart

A couple was getting on an elevator at a hotel. As they stepped in, the wife reminded the husband—"Floor 9." You'd think she had just given him a geography test. His finger was traveling all over the buttons looking for 9. I wanted to say, "It's between 8 and 10," but that would have been mean. His wife smiled, grabbed his arm tighter, and kissed his shoulder. "You're still thinking about that deal, aren't you?"

"Yeah."

"It'll work out."

Brain fog happens to all of us. This wife cherished her husband by not mentally ridiculing him (as I did), but thinking about him in a positive way—he's distracted, he's focusing somewhere else, but he's still an intelligent man. She chose to put a positive spin on the situation.

That's what cherishing calls us to do. For some of you, this will take a lot of practice. If you're naturally sarcastic or snide, you'll have to fight back your default mode of making a joke at your spouse's expense or demeaning them and instead choose to think the best of them. To do this, learn a simple trick: *Don't listen to yourself; talk to yourself.* Take control of your mind, reject the negative, and choose the positive.

Philippians 4:8 tells us that when we think about our spouses, we should focus on:

- whatever is true
- whatever is noble
- whatever is right
- whatever is pure
- whatever is lovely

- whatever is admirable
- whatever is excellent or praiseworthy

This calls you to take charge of your mind, to discipline it to dwell on the things about your spouse that are worthy of celebration. If when you think about your spouse you dwell on whatever is *not* honorable, whatever is distasteful, frustrating, shameful, and deserving of censure, don't be surprised if your heart follows.

I'm sure that man walked out of the elevator on the ninth floor feeling understood and cherished rather than embarrassed and disrespected. That's what every spouse should aim for.

2. Sacrifice for Your Spouse

Among the most patriotic citizens are active and retired soldiers. When you have fought for a flag, even risking your life, it makes the flag and what it represents even more precious to you.

The same is true in marriage. The more you invest in your spouse—your time, your emotions, your service, even your welfare—the more you will cherish him or her. Why? *Sacrifice shapes your heart.*

"James" loves craft beers; it's become a middle-aged hobby for him. He travels on a weekly basis and could easily indulge his hobby by checking out the myriad local breweries he comes across in the course of his business, but he doesn't, because he has promised his wife, "I won't drink when I'm not with you."

Drinking makes a person vulnerable when they're alone on the road. I don't know if there was a close call that elicited this policy, but James holds to his commitment, and guess what? It shapes his heart. Whereas drinking could make him forget who he is, not drinking (even though he wants to) makes him remember his wife. It helps him to cherish her as it brings her to his mind. He looks forward to returning home to her, as he not only gets to see her; he gets to engage in a favorite activity he'll do only when she is by his side. James gains more by sacrificing than he would by indulging; he has a marriage in the empty-nest years he finds truly satisfying.

If you wonder how sacrifice leads to cherish, consider this: who cherishes that first car more—the teenager who has one given to him or the young man who worked evenings and weekends and saved money for three years to purchase it on his own?

Sacrifice lays the groundwork for a cherishing mind-set. Try it, and you'll see.

3. Hug Liberally

An Italian publisher invited Lisa and me to a conference in Italy to help launch the Italian publication of three of my books. It was astonishing on our first night there to watch so much hugging and kissing. A woman walked up to our table, and our host's face lit up. He was beaming as he grabbed her and kissed her and excitedly (one would presume; I don't speak Italian) asked her how she was doing.

She must be someone quite close to him, I thought.

But over the next thirty minutes, we found out there were a lot of people who were "quite close" to him! Everyone got an enthusiastic, touching welcome. And most of the people at the conference did the same. Fathers were affectionate with sons; friends were affectionate with friends; people got kissed, hugged, and verbally greeted with enthusiasm all week long.

It made me think how little my kids and wife got touched and hugged in comparison. I always hug them when I see them and watch them leave. But this was a communal hug and kiss. Not just the parent, but seemingly everyone. And I wonder how emotionally starved many North American spouses and children are from not making someone's face light up when they are greeted or when they aren't touched beyond an occasional cold handshake or fist bump.

Since coming back from Italy, I've noticed something: taking an extra thirty to forty-five seconds to prolong my morning hug with Lisa does wonders. I used to hug Lisa after she woke up almost like we were just passersby—"good morning"—and then go about my day since I was usually already up and running. Taking just an extra thirty seconds makes the hug feel qualitatively different to Lisa; it increases its impact by 100 percent and makes her feel cherished. I'm not just loving her out of obligation; I'm cherishing her with delight.

Neurologically, hugging releases oxytocin into our brain. Oxytocin is a neuropeptide, often called the "cuddle chemical," that promotes "feelings of devotion, trust and bonding," according to DePauw University psychologist Matt Hertenstein. Dr. Hertenstein told NPR that hugging "really lays the biological foundation and structure for connecting to other people."[23]

In other words, we can use our arms to shape our brains so cherishing becomes our default response.

4. Need Your Spouse

One of the best ways to cherish your spouse is to need him or her and to let them know it. My wife doesn't want to feel kept or even cherished, if by cherish you mean treating her like a fragile porcelain doll on a pedestal. She wants to feel *valuable*. Feeling valuable is what makes her feel cherished.

We all want to be needed, and if we feel like we're not, we won't feel cherished.

Alex is an only-born, and his personality is true to birth order. He's an in-charge kind of guy who handles everything. He married Amy, who as a lastborn was used to and liked being taken care of.* Through a long series of events, including some serious medical scares, God took Alex's feet out from under him. He was laid out, unable to keep up with his business and home responsibilities, and Amy had to step up.

Over the course of the next several months, Amy discovered she *liked* having a lot of responsibility. When she made a business choice Alex wouldn't have made and it turned out she was right, she relished the expression on Alex's face. When Alex was able to return to work, the business and the house were both better off than when he went into the hospital.

Even more profound for Amy was what this hiatus did for their marriage. Being needed made Amy feel cherished. And needing Amy made Alex cherish her more. He appreciated and respected Amy on a deeper and broader level.

Remember when God cherished Jerusalem in Ezekiel 16? His cherishing turned Jerusalem, an abandoned orphan, into a royal queen who became world-famous. A queen isn't an empty celebrity who spends all her time taking selfies and posting them on the Internet; a queen *rules*.

No spouse wants to feel inept or "kept" in any arena of life.

---

* I'm not saying all only-borns and lastborns are like this, just that Alex and Amy fit the stereotype for what firstborns and lastborns are typically like.

If you never let your husband or wife "need" you, they'll never truly feel cherished.

When God gave Adam a helper, it wasn't just because he was lonely; it was because he needed help. Marriage isn't solely a cure for loneliness; it's also very much about two people supporting and helping each other.

Some of you run yourselves ragged because you don't want to "bother" your spouse. You don't realize that an occasional "hey, I really need you to help me with this" can be a gift of affirmation.* It validates your spouse's worth. It can make them feel cherished. Plus, it trains your brain to cherish your spouse in return.

5. Recognize Your Spouse's Royalty

Another method of maintaining a cherishing attitude for your spouse is to honor him or her for their *position*. Prince George gets a lot of press, though he hasn't accomplished anything. As the son of William and Kate, he is filled with royal blood and therefore commands attention.

Spiritually speaking, you married a royal spouse. Traditional Eastern Orthodox weddings celebrate a practice called "crowning." The bride and groom wear crowns as part of the festivities. In days long past, an Eastern Orthodox bride and groom wore those crowns for eight days following the ceremony. Far more typical today, the crowns are removed at the end of the ceremony.

A truly Christian marriage places us in a long order of "royal couples," descending from Adam and Eve (the first ones told to "rule over . . . every living creature that moves on the ground"

---

* I realize some of you have said this and found that your spouse didn't step up and maybe even resented it. That's an entirely different dynamic than what I'm addressing here.

[Genesis 1:28]), Abraham and Sarah, Isaac and Rebekah, Jacob and Rachel, David and Bathsheba, Zechariah and Elizabeth, and Joseph and Mary. It's a recognition that Christian marriage is about more than happiness and children; it's about testifying to God's long-term plan to bring humanity back after the fall to reclaim God's world through the Messiah. We are royal representatives through whom God spreads his reign and builds his kingdom.

After writing about God's long-term plan of redemption, the apostle Peter proclaims, "You are a chosen people, a royal priesthood, a holy nation, God's special possession, that you may declare the praises of him who called you out of darkness into his wonderful light" (1 Peter 2:9). This is the context that precedes what Peter says to wives (3:1–6) and husbands (3:7). It's a clear statement that we are to treat each other in light of *our spiritual royalty*. Our marriages are about more than each other; they are about testifying to God's kingdom—a mission served in part by recognizing the royal place each partner has in that kingdom.

When a princess misbehaves, she is still a princess and entitled to a certain respect. When a prince has a bad day, he doesn't lose his royal blood.

Consider the case of Terry, a delightful man from Winnipeg, who has had two loves and two heartbreaks. Both of his wives died of illness. His first wife died after twenty-one years of marriage; his second wife, Sharon, died after seventeen years of marriage.

His life of two marriages offers a test case for cherishing a spouse. The main difference in Terry's second marriage from his first, in his own words, is that Terry called Sharon "princess" and then treated her like one.

Terry's first wife died from ovarian cancer. The disease

unleashed a terrible five-year battle, and the last eight months required around-the-clock care. Terry got used to doing everything and getting almost nothing in return. This was new for him, but what else can you do when your wife is slowly dying from a horrible disease?

Terry remarried four years after his first wife died. Because the last years of his marriage had required him to do most of the daily chores and then his four years of singleness required him to do everything on his own, he maintained the same attitude with his second marriage. Sharon had been single for forty-four years before she married Terry, and having a man serve her like Terry did when she was used to being on her own made her feel like the luckiest woman in the world.

Terry says his second marriage was much closer and in many ways much richer than his first marriage, not because one woman was more excellent than another, but because his *attitude* about marriage was so dramatically different. He treated his wife like she was royalty. How would you treat a queen? That's how Terry treated Sharon.

Cherishing Sharon this way gave Terry a heart that made him cherish Sharon all the more. The more he served her and protected her, the more he cherished her. That's why he called her princess up until the day she died.

I pressed Terry on this just to make sure I understood him correctly. He had two marriages, one much closer than the other. But the difference wasn't the excellence of one wife over another (which is what we usually think generates marital happiness). The difference was his attitude toward one wife over another. He was committed to and loved his first wife, but he cherished his second wife.

Terry's story of two different marriages shows how much of an impact a commitment to cherishing can make. Terry's life tells us it's not so much about who we marry as it is about how we act in marriage and the attitude we maintain toward our spouses in marriage.

6. Make Your Spouse's Dreams Come True

In general, cherish is built on small, steady affirmations. To truly cherish someone, however, means, at least a couple times, you want to go large.

We've all read about children facing a terminal illness who were given special fantasy fulfillment days—meeting a famous athlete, going to a theme park, etc. I've heard of spouses who, when receiving their partner's terminal medical diagnosis, planned to finally make a long-delayed fantasy come true.

Why not start planning that fantasy now?

Husbands, the most common fantasy I hear from wives is actually . . . Europe. So many wives have mentioned how, when the kids are gone or money isn't so tight, they'd love to visit Paris or London or some other favored European city. If you're living on a middle-class income, traveling to Europe may seem so outside the realm of possibility that you just say, "Yeah, it'd be nice."

But what if you could save $500 to $700 a year secretly (that's about $50 to $80 a month)? In a decade, you'd have enough to fund a decent vacation to Europe. Imagine how your wife's face would light up when she opens a present with a picture of the Eiffel Tower on which you've written, "Our Next Date Night." Imagine how much more it will mean that you sacrificed for so long—for more than a decade—taking money out of your own discretionary spending to make one of her lifelong dreams come true.

And here's the thing: the *process* of secretly saving up and even sacrificing to make her dream become a reality will dramatically shape your heart and mind toward increasingly cherishing your spouse. Adopting the attitude of "I don't care what breaks and needs repairing, this secret stash of money is not going to be raided; nothing is more important than making my wife's dream come true" will reinforce your desire for her.

You may only be able to make a long-term wish like this happen once or twice in the course of your marriage, but shouldn't you at least try once or twice?

Besides, this is one of the best uses of money you'll ever find. A study at San Francisco State University found that while most people felt money spent on physical products was better spent than money spent on experiential activities, using money to purchase experiences with loved ones actually led to more overall happiness than purchasing physical products: "The study demonstrates that experiential purchases, such as a meal out or theater tickets, result in increased well-being because they satisfy higher order needs."[24]

For others of you, your spouse's lifelong dream might not be a place to visit, but a place to work. When Donnie and Jaclyn lived in Nashville, they had so little money that they qualified for food stamps. Jaclyn was pursuing a career in photography, which can take a long time to launch, and she started to feel guilty about not contributing more to the family budget.

One of her good friends worked as a waitress at a restaurant, and Jaclyn thought maybe she should do that as well.

"No, you're *not* doing that," Donnie said with uncharacteristic force. "Keep pursuing your photography. One day, it's going to become lucrative. I just know it."

Donnie explains his thinking: "I grew up hearing women talk about giving up their dreams once they got married, and that's not what I wanted for Jaclyn. I didn't care what her dream was, to be honest. If she wanted to be a stay-at-home mom, if she wanted to get a master's degree, or if she wanted to pursue a career in photography, I was determined to help make it happen."

This commitment came at great cost to Donnie. He had to work two jobs to make up for lack of income from Jaclyn's employment. When Jaclyn got her first bite at a commercial job, she didn't have the right equipment and was planning to pass up the opportunity, but Donnie bought her a two-thousand-dollar camera lens so she would have the tools she needed.

"And this was when we really didn't have twenty dollars to buy groceries."

Today, Jaclyn *does* have a lucrative photography business. Billboards all over Houston feature some of her work. In fact, she has a lot of other photographers working for her now. "I pay them to do most of the shooting, and I do a lot of the editing now."

Even more than what this sacrificial attitude did for Donnie and Jaclyn's bank account, however, is what it did for their marriage. Jaclyn feels cherished. She's the one who said in the first chapter of this book, "Sometimes I feel guilty that we have it so good."

7. Watch and Delight

A national marriage ministry invited Lisa and me to enjoy a small-boat cruise without being asked to speak even once.

"We just want to thank you for the investment you make in so many marriages," we were told.

Lisa and I enjoyed getting to focus on doing fun things on excursions without my having to prepare for anything later in the day. I was able to be more present as a husband instead of being preoccupied about what I was going to say in an evening talk.

Perhaps that's why I was able to be doubly delighted the first day on board. Lisa is the queen of travel plans and excursions, and she loves it. She will study options, look up reviews, compare prices, and come up with stuff that 95 percent of us would miss. True to form, she had done her research before we even got on the boat. As we sat on that first evening in the common area where the excursions were listed in a notebook, Lisa became the de facto cruise entertainment director. She got asked one question and answered it so well that someone else asked another and then another, and soon there was a circle around her. I watched, fascinated, as Lisa shone.

Our kids and I sometimes laugh at Lisa's plans for vacations, but here others were enjoying her gifts as well. She was on center stage, my ballerina, and others were benefiting from something I've learned to take for granted.

There are so many adorable aspects of Lisa that it's easy for me to forget just how helpful, practical, and intelligent she can be. Sitting back and watching her in action recharged my cherishing mind and heart. I just watched and marveled and cherished.

Sometimes you have to take a step back, observe, and even meditate on your spouse. Look at your spouse in an impressive situation like it's the first time you've seen them. *Remind your mind why you fell in love in the first place.* When you do that, cherish will naturally follow.

8. Conserve Your Energy

By now, you've surely come to understand that all this cherishing business takes a lot of time, effort, energy, and thought. You can become infatuated with a boyfriend or girlfriend by accident, but you can't accidentally cherish a spouse. Cherishing takes intention, purpose, and reflection if it's going to last. I asked one wife what made her feel most cherished, and her one-word answer was "intention."

Learning to cherish your spouse is one reason you have to avoid addictions or continue to work faithfully in recovery if you are already addicted. Addictions war against cherishing. They sap the energy you should be expending on your marriage. You can feed an addiction or you can feed your marriage, but you can't feed both. One or the other will go hungry.

This is true even of "healthy" addictions. Some women, without realizing it, can't help but put their mothering duties above being a wife. To live any other way would feel forced, painful, and even unthinkable—which pretty much makes parenting sound like an addiction. The same could be said of jobs, hobbies, or pleasing our parents. I have seen marriages grow more and more distant when a woman starts thinking about and living for running marathons; a man is obsessed with growing his church; a woman can't think about anything except getting her kids to be successful; a man plots ways to be alone to indulge his electronic fantasies. Every second given over to something else is a second stolen from our spouses.

To live lives of cherishing our spouses, we must be wary of cherishing too much of something else. We cannot live with appropriate intensity for our spouses if we are pouring ourselves out on something else. And let me say, I've never seen anything else be as satisfying as an intimate marriage marked by cherishing each other.* I've run a dozen marathons, including qualifying for three Boston Marathons, and sometimes at the end of these, I still think, *What's the point?*

Few things last in life like marriage. You can pour yourself out on behalf of your kids, but if they're emotionally and physically healthy, they're eventually going to leave your home and start lives of their own. No man in the history of the universe has ever been satisfied living a life driven by alcohol dependency or the adrenaline rush of gambling. Each one of these brings far more misery than satisfaction into the human soul.

What I'm saying is that for your own happiness and satisfaction, be wary of the solitary pursuits and energies that steal the joy and wonder of being in a marriage in which you truly cherish each other. It's natural and even healthy to have outside passions that your spouse may not share, but put a check on the time and energy you devote to them. You cannot cherish your spouse if you are obsessed with pleasing yourself.

The End Result

Lisa and I visited a small, funky southern California beach town one afternoon and stopped at a restaurant—which Lisa had dutifully researched—for lunch.

"Let's go for a walk," Lisa said as soon as we finished.

---

* According to Matthew 6:33, our first pursuit should be the kingdom of God, even above intimacy in marriage. So I'm writing this in that context. However, as I argue in *A Lifelong Love*, loving my spouse—God's daughter—is an aspect of that kingdom. Even so, the best, most intimate marriages will be unified pursuits of kingdom work, not focused even primarily on each other. So please read these words with that caveat in mind.

Cherish

Two blocks later, the harshest-sounding metallic crash I'd ever heard in my life thundered all around us. Lisa flinched, and I jumped over her, putting her in front of me and somewhat underneath me. We paused and waited for just a second, wondering what was to come next, when I looked back and saw there had been an accident at a construction site.

It wasn't a bomb or an act of terrorism.

It was just a *very loud* drop.

"Ahhhh, you saved my life," Lisa kidded.

I didn't have time to think. All I knew was that something potentially threatening was happening behind us, and I instinctively put myself between whatever was threatening us and Lisa. It was a split-second reaction.

What happened? I've been praying to cherish Lisa. I've been choosing to cherish Lisa. For three decades, I've asked God to give me a heart to cherish Lisa as God's Son cherishes the church. So when something occurred that bypassed the rational process, I had no time to think, but just to react—I saw that God had indeed shaped my heart, and I chose to protect and cherish. Neuroplasticity in action!

Here's what was curious: for the rest of the day, I felt an even more intense love for Lisa, like we were teenagers. I was slightly scared—she could have been hurt! And I felt so tender toward her, so affectionate. I didn't want to let her out of my sight.

This cherishing stuff *works*.

⟨ CHERISHING CHERISH ⟩

- Cherish is a chosen mental attitude; once set in motion, it can eventually become our default mode of action, but there are things we can do to set that up.

- Think about your spouse's positive qualities.

- The more we sacrifice for our spouses, the more we tend to cherish them.

- Hugs and touching are tools to help us cherish our spouses more.

- We cherish what we need. Find ways to "need" your spouse. Let them serve you.

- Recognize your spouse's spiritual royalty. Terry discovered that his second marriage was superior to his first in terms of happiness and intimacy because of his attitude, not because of his spouse.

- Discover one of your spouse's big dreams and start making the small choices necessary to pull off a long-term plan, even if it will take more than a decade. The mere practice of saving up will create a cherishing mind-set.

- Watch and delight. Sit back and drink it in when your spouse is being showcased.

- Conserve your energy. An overly busy life and an addicted life are both enemies of mental cherishing.

QUESTIONS FOR DISCUSSION AND REFLECTION

1. What one or two strategies can you employ to train your mind to think positively about your spouse?

2. What has cherishing your spouse cost you lately? If you can't think of anything you've had to sacrifice, what can you do to sacrifice on their behalf in the next week or two?

3. What kind of (nonsexual) touch makes your spouse feel cherished? What kind of touch makes you feel cherished? How can you remind yourself to hug or touch throughout the day?

4. Talk about how husbands and wives might treat each other differently in private, in front of the kids, and out in public if they truly respected each other's spiritual royalty.

5. What can couples in their first marriages learn from Terry's experience of having been in two marriages? How can couples start over with new attitudes so they can deepen their present marriages?

6. How valuable do you think your spouse feels to you? What can you do to increase their sense of feeling valuable?

7. What lifelong bucket-list items does your spouse have? Which one of them could you begin planning to make come true?

8. What keeps you from conserving your mental energy so you have something left over to cherish your spouse? What can you do to cut back on it so you can start a new life of mentally choosing to cherish your spouse?

CHAPTER 12

Easier to Cherish

Making it easier for our spouses to cherish us

A ll of us want to be cherished, and the truth is, if I want my wife to cherish me, the best path to get there is to work on becoming someone who is easier to cherish.

If as you read this book you've been wishing your spouse would treat you like I'm urging us to treat each other, ask yourself this question: *How can I make myself a little easier to cherish?* If we want to be cherished by someone, doesn't it make sense to focus on growing in areas that are easier to cherish while also growing out of patterns that make cherishing us particularly difficult? You may be tempted to say, "But he [she] is just supposed to cherish me, regardless"—and in a sense, you'd be right. In another sense, though, you're not really living in the real world.

The best things in life—and all change—start with humility.

The Neighborhood I Live In

I've said before that I'm not clinically OCD, but I live in the neighborhood right next to it. I have my routines I cherish and even guard. And that puts stress on Lisa. Cherishing my routines makes it more difficult for me to cherish Lisa and for Lisa to cherish me. I didn't understand in the early days of our marriage how Lisa's upsetting my routines sent my stress levels through the roof. That's my issue, not hers, but I used to think it was hers.

This has been a lifelong problem, and we're still dealing with it. Just this past year—three decades in!—my wife and I were visiting our son and his new wife at their apartment in Seattle. I used to love running around Green Lake when we lived in the Pacific Northwest, but since it's almost eighty miles from where we lived in Bellingham, I usually ran there while driving back from the airport. My son now lived in an apartment less than a quarter mile away. How many times had I run around Green Lake and then had to sit in wet, sweaty running clothes as I drove back to our home where I could take a shower? Many times. But now I knew someone with a shower just a couple blocks away!

I couldn't wait to experience a Green Lake run and not have to pay for it by sitting in sweaty clothes.

It was a Sunday. We had gone to our son's church that morning and were planning the rest of our day. I was scheduled to run ten miles that day. (It's a joke to call it "scheduled"—I don't have a coach and no one is checking on me, but I had it in my mind that I "needed" to run at least ten miles that day. No, I can't defend it. That's the mind I live with.) As we discussed the day's activities, I kept coming back to when I could fit my run in.

Very patiently and lovingly, Lisa finally said, "Gary, maybe that's not the first concern right now. Let's figure out these other things. Would it be all that terrible if you ran a shorter distance today and did ten miles tomorrow?"

I realized what I was doing—obsessing compulsively—and

I don't want to be that way. Lisa was helping me see what I was doing, and I was grateful for it, because I truly want to be more like Jesus. Jesus is a servant. He's not driven by compulsive, fake "needs." (For the record, I *did* get my ten miles in around Green Lake, with a wonderful portion of it next to my son.)

If you want to be cherished, practice humility and admit there are some really irritating parts of you that need to be transformed—and *welcome the transformation*. In your head, you know you are not perfect, right? But how we resent it when our spouses see that even more clearly than we do and point it out.

The divide between that hypocritical gap can be called "pride."

Here's what's *not* helpful: trying to overcome the divide by thinking our spouses have the problem instead of us. We do this quite cleverly, saying, "He [she] is just overreacting." Instead of us having a problem, the problem is our spouses' overreactions to the problem! And then we get a friend or extended family member to confirm that our spouses are being too hard on us. If you want to become someone who is more cherishable, you have to realize your friend's or extended family member's opinion of you isn't as valid as your spouse's—for this reason, as Tim Keller puts it: "While your character flaws may have created mild problems for other people, they will create major problems for your spouse and your marriage . . . No one else is as inconvenienced and hurt by your flaws as your spouse is. And therefore your spouse becomes more keenly aware of what is wrong with you than anyone else ever has been."[25]

It's one thing to "visit" a character flaw; it is another thing entirely to live with a character flaw. Just because something about you doesn't bother a friend, a parent, or a sibling, it doesn't mean your spouse is overreacting when it bothers them. Marriage amplifies everything—sometimes for good and sometimes for bad.

Pause for a moment and list three things that might make it more difficult for someone to cherish you:

_____

_____

_____

If something I do is really bugging my spouse and I want an intimate, "connected" marriage, then that's all the motivation I should need to get more serious about addressing it. The fact that it doesn't bug my brother or my best friend is irrelevant, because I'm not trying to build a marriage with my brother or best friend. I'm trying to build a marriage with my spouse, and if my obsessiveness is getting in the way, then I need to be humble, honest, and ruthless with that weakness.

In my blog, some personality types push back vigorously against this notion: "You're asking me to become someone different. My spouse should accept me as I am." My answer is twofold. First, Jesus (Matthew 5:48), Paul (2 Corinthians 7:1), Peter (2 Peter 1:5–9), James (1:4), and John (1 John 3:2–3) all call us to become something we're not—i.e., to *grow*. No one would need to grow if they were already perfect. If your spouse is calling you into a greater degree of Christlikeness, he or she is acting as God's servant to help you apply teaching from every major New Testament writer/teacher.

Second, by allowing myself to be transformed through marriage, I am merely exchanging a selfish and stubborn independence for the amazing reality of being intimately known, loved, and cherished. I've lived both lives, and I think connected intimacy is much better than fierce, independent defensiveness. If I have to die to a few self-centered things to get to a much better place, all in all that's a rather cheap ticket to happiness.

Humility calls us to be thankful—not resentful or defensive—for a spouse who knows how to handle the irritating points of our personality with grace, courage, and gentleness.

Help Me

Another way to help your spouse learn to cherish you is to welcome their assistance in helping you become a more effective *servant* in God's kingdom. Again, humility is paramount. To become more effective means, by definition, that we're not yet as effective as we might be.

In their bestseller *Building Your Mate's Self-Esteem*, Barbara Rainey writes about encouraging Dennis in the early days of his speaking ministry. Dennis freely admits English wasn't his best subject (fishing was), so his early talks usually contained several glaring grammatical errors.

Barbara understands how grammar is supposed to work and thus pointed out several of Dennis's mistakes. Dennis later asked Barbara to be careful about when she shared these constructive critiques (i.e., not right after he was done), but he listened—and look at what has happened: Dennis is now one of the premier communicators for marriage and family in the world. He receives all kinds of esteem, and rightfully so, because his daily words reach millions of people.

Dennis was willing to become better at speaking, so now it's even easier for his wife to cherish him. How could she not be proud of him as she sees how God has used him? If he had resisted her efforts to help him, he would have remained a less-effective communicator.

If your wife can help you with time management; if your husband can offer some tips for negotiating; if your spouse can offer some insight into how you can be more effective in your job or social relationships, hear them out. Listen. Saying you could be even more effective doesn't mean they don't respect you. It just means we're all human and can do even better. And it makes you easier to cherish. Paul urged Timothy to let everyone see his *progress* (1 Timothy 4:15). Every one of us is a *growing* Christian, not yet arrived.

It's a fine line—you want to be cherished and accepted as you are (an understandable desire), but don't you also want to improve so you can be even more *authentically* cherished? The more you listen to your spouse, the easier you make it for your spouse to cherish you.

Living Large

Dennis's story points to another aspect of becoming more cherishable: he lives for a purpose outside himself. The best thing you can do to raise your esteem in the eyes of your spouse is to offer yourself to God and begin living for others. When you share your gifts and talents with others, it's inspiring. When someone inspires you, it's easier to cherish them.

N. T. Wright tells of a gifted art student at Oxford who became a believer, and his tutors despised him for it. He later began painting abstract icons that were so spectacular and brilliant that these same tutors began raving about his fresh creativity. In a sense, they began to cherish him more as a student. He waited until they saw the results before telling them that these new paintings were actually icons inspired by his new faith.[26] He wasn't painting to be important or admired; he was painting to bring God-consciousness to the world. That's easy to cherish, whether you do it by teaching a history class, being a police officer, a high school guidance counselor, or a small business owner. Don't make your vocation just about you; get lost in the larger picture of God's reaching the world in the corner he's entrusted to you.

What I want to cherish in my wife isn't fading beauty, worldly fame, economic security, or respect from society. I'll cherish a woman who is devoted to her family, to her God, to making a difference in eternity. A woman who worships rather than worries. A woman who is deliberate and focused rather than just busy. A woman who pursues peace, humility, gentleness, and patience more than she pursues comfort and affluence. A woman who seeks to spread faith rather than manipulate wealth. A woman who impresses others with the truth of the gospel rather than seeks to impress them with her appearance.

This is an easy woman to cherish because living for God, and then living for others, is noble. It's inspiring. It's something to celebrate.

It is a holy prayer to say, "God, please start using me. You created me for a purpose. You saved me for a mission. Help me to understand and to begin fulfilling that mission."

One of the practical things this does is give the two of you something to talk and pray about. Shared ministry accomplishes the same thing that combat does for soldiers or competition does for teammates—it binds us together in a common endeavor. It is a tall order to stay enthralled with each other—we're just too common, and we grow so familiar with each other—but it is never less than exciting to see God move among his people. God isn't common, and his creative ways never become overly familiar. Our hearts never lose the wonder of seeing him move yet again. If you find yourself listless in your marriage, the cure is usually seeking more of God. One of the best things you can do to renew or revive a marriage is to start focusing on God's work outside your marriage.

If you have no sense of call or mission from God, your first step in becoming a person who is easier to cherish is to seek God and find a place to begin serving.*

Consider Your Spouse

Wives, in an earlier chapter, we spoke to your husbands about cherishing your body and about praying that God would make you their standard of beauty. Women usually love it when I talk to their husbands about this. But here's the thing: if you want to make it easier for him to do this, you've got to consider some of what attracted him to you.

Men, if your wife fell in love with a fitness buff who then traded in cardio workouts for nachos, we can't expect her to not notice. Weight gain is inevitable for the vast majority of us. There are a few freaks of nature who manage to cheat normal physiology, but if our spouses chose us as people who at least valued fitness and were generally engaged in life but then became someone almost entirely different, a couch potato who

---

* In *A Lifelong Love*, I talk about couples discovering their mission in a chapter titled "Got Mission?" Dennis and Barbara Rainey have an excellent chapter, "What Is Your Destiny?" in their book *The New Building Your Mate's Self-Esteem* ([Nashville: Nelson, 1995], 219–34). If you're struggling with how to define and understand your mission, check out these chapters.

steadily withdraws from life, we are making huge demands on their charity.

Once we get married, our bodies aren't entirely our own. If we want to be cherished, we should hold this reality as a trust rather than independently stake our claim and tell our spouses to just deal with it.

I can't tell you how many times I've heard the story: guy meets girl with long flowing hair; they fall in love; she has a baby or two; and then she surprises him with a short, "cute" haircut that all her girlfriends rave about.

It's sensible and easier to care for. It's *adorable*.

And the first time her husband sees it, even if he's a master poker player, he can't hide his disappointment.

Does it matter as much if every one of your girlfriends, your mom, and your sisters agree that the shorter hair is so wonderful when your husband tries to hide his disappointment? I'm not saying every guy will be disappointed. Maybe your particular husband loves shorter hair. And I'm not saying he gets to choose.

I'm *not* saying that.

Here's what I *am* saying: how much thought are you giving to the guy who fell in love with you and the way you look?

For years, I fought male-pattern baldness, always telling my wife to let me know when it was time to admit defeat and just shave it off. One man started talking to me a decade ago about how good the hairpieces are these days, but I think you can eventually tell when someone goes that route, and I find it difficult to reconcile trying to communicate the truth of God to the world when my head is a lie.

Finally, one morning Lisa looked at me and said, "Gary, it's time."

I liked having hair. I liked the feel and smell of shampooing. But Lisa looks at my head more often than I do, so I went in *that day* and got it done.

So this isn't just about you, women. I can't fool myself. All things being equal, the vast majority of women (including my wife) would prefer a man with hair. There are some things we can't change. But we can be sensitive to the things we *can* change. When sickness or age forces a radical change in appearance, mature, godly spouses will increase their affection and cherishing. It's the *attitude* I'm talking about, not the externals. Though we can't stop many of the effects of aging, we can at least take our spouses' preferences to heart and make it a little easier for them to cherish the way we look.

Meeting the Need

One of the quickest ways to increase your spouse's desire to cherish you is to find a need and meet it.

You could describe my bond with my iPad as emotional. I traveled for years without one, and when the first model came out, I thought it was nothing but a toy. A couple years later, I bought one and discovered how much easier it is to use an iPad when speaking than paper notes. It's also so much easier to check email on it than firing up a laptop, and the map app works especially well for this directionally challenged man, with a screen my aging eyes can actually see. Good night! I all but fell in love, if it's possible to do that with an electronic gadget.

When something meets a need, it's usually cherished.

Once we became empty nesters, Lisa began working much more actively with what I do. For a period of time, we didn't have anyone to oversee our website, and I'm way down there as far as tech knowledge goes. I felt vulnerable every day, but people we contracted with kept quitting, and I just didn't have the time to find out who could work with me. I was traveling alone, working many thirteen- or fourteen-hour days when in Houston, and I always intended to get to a more permanent website fix but just couldn't.

So I lived with an extreme vulnerability. I could wake up any morning and the website could be toast—and then I'd be stranded.

Finally, after about a month, Lisa stepped in, found a great solution, and told me they had already backed up the website so if it crashed, nothing would be lost.

"You mean you're supposed to back it up?" I asked, realizing for the first time we had been far more vulnerable than I realized.

The way Lisa stepped in warmed my middle-aged heart as much as anything she could have done. I had a great need, she met it, and I was extremely grateful.

You want to be cherished? Find a need like this and meet it. Write out three frustrations you know your spouse struggles with. What can you do to alleviate these frustrations? It helps to set a deadline.

_____

_____

_____

Letting Yourself Be Cherished

Some of you make it difficult for your spouse to cherish you because you won't allow yourself to be cherished. In fact, if this is you, everything I've said in this chapter may actually be *harmful.* You fall into an entirely different category: those who need to surrender to the spiritual truth that you are cherishable just the way you are.

My friend Dr. Steve Wilke has spent more than thirty years counseling couples and families. He estimates that about one-third of the couples in churches today have at least one spouse who has experienced some type of trauma that makes them feel uncherishable. "It's one of Satan's strategies to derail an individual from both receiving grace and God's love and, by definition, love from all others," Wilke says.

Another way to put this is that Satan wants to make your hurt *last.* He wants to extend it. He wants to take something terrible that happened to you in your past and make it something terrible that robs you of joy and peace in your present and future.

According to Dr. Wilke, "The trauma could be from childhood, adulthood, or even PTSD from the battlefield."

Megan had been in a severely abusive eleven-year-long marriage that included emotional, mental, sexual, and physical abuse. "I thought that because I was a woman, I was God's afterthought, used-up and unloved, not valuable and not important, deserving of poor treatment."

When she met David, who was to become her new husband, she at first thought David was too good to be true. "Because of the abuse I suffered at the hands of my ex-husband, I really did not trust that a man could show affection and honor toward a woman without wanting something in return."

Early on in her marriage to David, Megan would sometimes jump when David touched her, afraid that he only wanted to use her (or, just as bad, harm her). David believed that "Megan had a deep capacity to love and to be loved, but it had all been stomped on and squashed down in her previous marriage, and allowing it all come to the surface again was not going to be easy for her. I could also tell it would be well worth the wait."

David excelled in cherishing Megan by giving her much time, soft touch, acceptance, and soft words. He didn't expect Megan to just "get over" her past experience, so he didn't take her flinches personally. He gently assured her that he didn't think any worse of her for how she was involuntarily reacting, while assuring her that he would never intentionally hurt or use her.

He also cherished Megan by valuing her thoughts. Says Megan, "He began to show me that my thoughts are precious and important and that he valued my input. He and I had long talks about who I am and who I am becoming. I eventually discovered that I wanted to pursue more education, start a nonprofit, and take a job that would enable me to offer kindness and mercy to hurting people."

One particularly significant night occurred at a restaurant called "The Rock." Old albums and posters of rock bands from every era hang on the walls, and music plays in the background. Megan loves the zucchini noodle dish ("healthy, spicy, and yummy!"), and that's what she was eating the night David put down his fork and patiently reminded Megan that she did not need to strive so hard to earn his love. "You are beautiful just as you are, and I just want to spend time in your presence."

This was overwhelming for Megan to hear. David's acceptance, his wanting to be with her, his enjoying her instead of being disappointed with her, even counting time with her as a gift, were foreign realities, but so healing and so wonderful.

"David asked me to quit working so hard and to simply *be*. I will never forget that conversation."

As a husband, David believes he benefited greatly from Megan's spiritual restoration. "Sometime later, after we were married, things got even better for us as a couple as she could actually *see* she was cherished indeed. I think part of the difference was that she had lived a couple of years of being truly treasured and cherished on a daily basis. Instead of having to *will* her total trust of me, she could trust me based on this practical and consistent cherishing of her that I had tried so intentionally to demonstrate. She actually believed she was beautiful to me. She could see she was valuable in my life and in the lives of so many other people. It was now evident to her that the Lord has a high plan for her, and that her life was not just a prop for someone else. When she began to see her actual worth, and that I as a person and as her husband was genuinely a better person because of who she was, our relationship went to another level in terms of intimacy, joy, and mutual contentment."

David's acceptance and cherishing opened a door for God to speak to Megan of his love as well. "Because of David's loving me as I am and where I am, I began to understand God's love for me, even in my darkest times. I started to bloom in our relationship, and I quit trying to earn David's love and God's love. I am important to him, and I am a priority.

"I'll never forget when David told me I am a priority to him. I cried when he went a step further and said, 'Megan, you are not only *a* priority; you are *the* priority.' That statement seemed to release my very soul! I believe I started soaring that day.

"David cherishes me. God cherishes me. The more I understand a deep and selfless love from David, the more I've been able to grasp the gospel. The more I can grasp the gospel, the more I can accept David's love. I only have one Savior and one Rescuer. But because of the ways in which David loved me, David gave me a deeper understanding of the Father-Friend who adores his girl."

Says David, "We have a wonderful marriage that continues to grow in love, trust, and intimacy like we have never experienced in our lives. It is a process, and at this point in time, Megan allows me to cherish and bless her without feeling guilty about it or wondering why I'm doing this for her. She knows I want to love her this way and that she is worth it and deserving of it."

Not Too Good to Be True

God's grace, acceptance, and affirmation in the face of our fallenness and rebellion sometimes seem too good to be true—but all these gifts of God are true. We have to accept them if we want to be cherished by our spouses. I sometimes hate being an imperfect husband. Even more, I loathe not being able to choose which weaknesses I manifest: "Okay, God, I'll sin that way, but not the other way."

If only.

If we believe God doesn't love the imperfect us, we'll never allow our spouses to love the imperfect us either.

Many of you have been hurt, but grace is God's remedy to make that hurt part of a painful past rather than a present reality. Let God's forgiveness, affirmation, and acceptance wash over you so you can receive your spouse's cherishing as a reflection of divine favor.

King David, a prideful adulterer and murderer, still understood God's *delight*. He uttered both of these statements:

- "He [God] brought me out into a spacious place; he rescued me *because he delighted in me*" (2 Samuel 22:20, italics added).
- "The LORD be exalted, *who delights in the well-being of his servant*" (Psalm 35:27, italics added).

And in Ephesians 5:1, the apostle Paul calls followers of Christ "dearly loved children."

It is only by receiving God's divine acceptance that you can receive your spouse's acceptance. God's delight in you isn't based on your behavior—not even close. He often comforts us most when we have pushed him away. Nor is his delight based on an innate goodness or on our own likability—what a joke. It's based on our Advocate, Jesus Christ. Psychologically, nothing else would work. Most of us could not convince ourselves that we are naturally lovable or good or respectable enough that our spouses could cherish us at all times. I'm not delusional! But when we "get" the gospel, when we receive the spiritual inheritance of forgiveness and redemption and the acceptance that follows, we can learn to surrender to being cherished.

Pray these words out loud: "Lord, I surrender to being cherished. Your Word says you delight in me. I receive it. Your Word says I'm a dearly loved child. I accept your true declaration over my faulty self-loathing. I surrender to your grace. I surrender to the fact that because of Jesus, you cherish the imperfect me."

Receiving this acceptance fuels our astonishment of God's grace. I mess up but am wonderfully reminded that God has made provision for my messes. I get too busy, too independent, too needy, and too arrogant. God brings it to mind and simply says, after repentance has done its work, "I've covered that sin; put it behind you, and let's begin again."

Living in grace, life becomes a never-ending series of being astonished: "You've got that covered too? And *that*? Wow. Your grace stretches *this* far, even through middle age—when I should know better? How amazing. How utterly amazing!" *Instead of feeling bad about myself, I feel so good about God.*

To cherish is to live in, be covered by, and share in the grace of God. It is to walk in wonder that God's grace really is wide enough, high enough, and deep enough for every one of us.

Guilt-ridden spouse, please let your spouse cherish you. It's the "Christian" thing to do!

CHERISHING CHERISH

- If we want to be cherished, one of the most effective ways is to humbly admit we need to grow in areas that make it easier for our spouses to cherish us.

- Our character weaknesses and quirks affect our spouses more than anyone else, which makes our spouses' opinions and preferences more important than anyone else's. This doesn't mean we bow to pathological or bent desires, of course, but it does mean that instead of insisting our spouses put up with obvious flaws, we demonstrate compassion and seek to address those flaws.

- We need to listen to our spouses' gentle corrections.

- We become more cherishable when we live a large life. The more selfish we are, the more difficult we make it for our spouses to cherish us.

- If you want your spouse to cherish you more, find a need and meet it.

- Remember the person your spouse fell in love with—consider their preferences before you make a radical change.

- Some of us don't feel cherished by our spouses because we won't allow ourselves to feel cherished by our spouses. This is a spiritual illness that requires a greater understanding and experience of God's grace.

QUESTIONS FOR DISCUSSION AND REFLECTION

1. Be honest: list three things that make it most difficult for your spouse to cherish you. Are you addressing these issues or just asking your spouse to put up with them?

2. In what ways have your character flaws and quirks brought great stress to your spouse?

3. Think of the last time your spouse corrected you. Laying aside the question of whether they did it in the right way, were you open to receiving it or did you become defensive?

4. Are you living a small life, focused on selfish concerns? How can you begin living larger? Have you thoughtfully considered how your unique gifts and personality can showcase God's love and light to the world?

5. Go back to the list of three needs your spouse has

right now. What can you do in the coming weeks to address these needs?

6. When it comes to physical appearance, are you sensitive to your spouse's preferences?

7. Are you making it difficult for your spouse to cherish you by feeling as if you're unworthy of being cherished? How can a better understanding of the gospel help you grow in this area? Ask others to recommend books that have helped them think more biblically in this area.

CHAPTER 13

Biblical Power to Keep On Cherishing

How understanding the truth about God's grace gives us the motivation and power to keep cherishing our spouses

Y ou don't stink so much for being a fat girl."

Yeah, Julie's father actually said that.

For the record, Julie isn't fat. She's not skinny, but no personal trainer or physician would ever call her fat. Her dad probably didn't think she was either; it was just his allegedly "humorous" way to remind his daughters to be careful—they were always on the edge of not quite being good enough.

Her dad's military bearing and view of tough love meant that excelling was expected and average was failing. One of Julie's siblings might as well get arrested as bring home a "C" on a report card—given the way their father looked at it.

Her mom's relationship with Julie's dad could be characterized by fear and dependence. She would never question her husband, his words, or his decisions. Her daughters had no protection against her husband's expectations.

Needless to say, Julie never felt cherished growing up. She is intelligent, attractive, and witty, but for decades she lived on the edge of a precipice without a net below to catch her—if she disappointed her parents, if she didn't live up to her best, she would fall into failure (and therefore insignificance), with no one to catch her.

And then she met and married Jeff.

Becoming Her Dad

Julie's heart eventually reawakened when God gave her a son who couldn't measure up to his sisters. Julie's oldest daughter might be president of the United States someday. Her second daughter is likely to take over Ford Motors. Her son, Brent? He has all the ambition of a retiree who owns a baseball card shop.

To make matters worse, Brent reminds Julie of Jeff. Jeff is a good man who loves the Lord and provides reasonably well for the family, contributing as much to the family income as does Julie. But he doesn't need to be in charge. He has no need to test himself by running marathons. He doesn't care if he drives a car that is ten years old. He doesn't care if the house needs a bit of patching up. He's more relational and sees home as a place where he can relate with loved ones, not a place to impress guests.

That's what attracted Julie to Jeff at first. She loved being so unconditionally accepted and adored, and she noticed a peace, contentment, and spiritual rest in Jeff that she fed off of.

Until, that is, they got married.

From that point on, Jeff could do almost nothing right.

Julie started off by asking him if he wanted to get more schooling. "Why?" Jeff asked. She may as well have asked him if he wanted to dye his hair orange. It sounded bizarre.

Then she started mentioning other employment opportunities. "But I like the people I work with," Jeff responded. "And I like my boss."

Julie finally accepted the fact that Jeff was content and even happy with a quiet life, but there was no way her son, Brent, was going to follow in his father's footsteps.

Until he did.

Brent is the mirror image of his father in temperament and physical appearance, so Julie set out to "save" him from Jeff's influence and help Brent live up to the potential of his sisters.

It took a friend to wake Julie up. "Julie," her friend said one day, "do you know how many wives envy you? Jeff is solid, kind, and thoughtful. He has helped so many people, and he makes them feel better about themselves while doing it. What Jeff lacks in ambition and income is more than covered by what he has in integrity, faith, relatability, and friendship. If you try to turn Brent into one of your daughters, you're going to ruin him. The world would be blessed to have another Jeff—and frankly, two of your daughters are probably enough."

Julie's friend was kinder, more thoughtful, and gentler in getting her point across than I've made it sound here, but Julie finally got the point: she was becoming her father.

Julie's friend said, her voice conveying compassion, "Julie, you've been a Christian your entire life. But I don't think you've ever understood the gospel."

"What are you talking about? I've been in church my entire life."

"Maybe so, but do you know what the gospel even means? Because I'm warning you: Brent and Jeff will never feel completely loved and accepted by you until you learn to let yourself be loved and accepted by God."

Grace is so foreign to us, so supernatural, so seemingly against logic, that it's not until we receive it from God that we can give it to others. Living in a fallen world, we will find it very difficult and at times even impossible to cherish others if we do not first receive grace, which is God's way of cherishing us. Grace is the gasoline that feeds the engine that drives our ability to cherish our spouses.

Three Truths

If you're unfamiliar with the word *gospel,* it means we are all sinners, invited through the kindness and generosity of God to be reconciled (brought into a right relationship) to him and saved from the righteous wrath of God (because we rebelled, didn't acknowledge him, went our own way, and brought great misery to God and others) through the applied death and resurrection of Jesus Christ. It's not something we earn; it's something we receive. That's what *gospel*—"good news"—means. (A little later in the chapter, we'll talk about an important second part—a "consequence" of the gospel.)

Our ability to keep on cherishing imperfect and sometimes ungrateful spouses—or even generally good, "average" spouses like Jeff—is dependent on understanding three basic gospel truths:

1. How much we ourselves have been forgiven.
2. What we've been saved from.

3. The cost Christ paid to win that salvation.

This will sound very religious to some of you. To others, it may sound overly familiar: "I already know that. I've heard this preached my whole life." But what we call the gospel message is the most practical help for your marriage you will ever find. It's also something we need to be reminded of just about every hour of every day if we want to keep on cherishing each other.

We're not empowered to cherish if we acknowledge the gospel as simply an historical truth. It has to be the moment-by-moment spiritual oxygen we breathe. It's such a powerful truth and we are such leaky vessels that the seemingly simple truth of living by this understanding may make this chapter the most impactful, helpful, and practical one yet.

If we don't seek to be recharged with this truth every day, I believe we will lose the power and motivation to cherish at a high intensity. This isn't an option for the most serious of believers; again, this is more like breathing. As soon as we let out one breath, we have to take in another breath.

If you get how sinful you are, if you truly understood the dark destiny that awaited you because of your sin, if you could glimpse just three seconds of the agonizing price Christ paid to give you something, not just pain-free, but glorious and rich, you'd serve others with joy for the rest of your life and smile while doing it. You're not doing God a favor by loving his son or his daughter. He did *you* a favor. What you're doing is nothing in comparison.

Practical, live-it-out-in-the-streets Christianity could almost (not quite, but almost) be reduced to this: because Christ served me, I now serve you.

If you don't understand your spiritual debt and original spiritual condition, you don't understand your salvation. If you do understand what you truly deserve, you'll never say, "I don't deserve this," as a complaint—those words will be uttered only as an astonished exclamation of gratitude.

"But I'm not that evil," you might say. That's like a high school basketball star feeling good about himself because he's never played against Stephen Curry. James grew up with Jesus, and this close proximity led him to conclude, "We all stumble in many ways" (James 3:2).* Having seen the moral excellence of Jesus firsthand, James couldn't pretend he was "all right." Seeing God in action made him realize just how far from perfect he (and all of us) really was. All of us, even the best of us on our best days, "stumble in many ways." (In context, James is referring to teachers and leaders.)

The act of winning us back from our stumbling didn't involve Jesus snapping his fingers, reciting a spell, and setting everything right. A price had to be paid. Jesus, the sinless one, became sin for us. We can't understand the spiritual agony of that sacrifice—an agony so great it probably killed him before the physical reality of the crucifixion did (Jesus' rather early death on the cross surprised the Roman authorities).

Once we accept the horror of what Jesus had to do because of what we couldn't do, we'll never resent dropping to our knees in the smallest act of service to others, beginning with our spouses.

But if you do understand the violent wickedness of your heart apart from God, the unending tortuous ruin of eternal

---

* Protestants believe Mary was the mother of James so that James grew up in the same house as Jesus. Roman Catholics typically believe James was a cousin. At any rate, they shared a childhood in close proximity.

separation from God, the heroic, certain, and costly victory of Jesus over sin and death given by grace to you—you'll look for ways to show your love extravagantly.

Because Christ served me, I now serve you.

Gladly.

With joy.

Without resenting the price.

If you spend every second of the rest of your life serving him, you won't come close to repaying the debt he paid on your behalf.

Because Julie believed she had earned her acceptance the hard way, she thought others needed to earn her acceptance as well. In her mind, she wasn't asking anything more of others than she had asked of herself.

The problem is, her standards were too low! She thought a surface discipline and ambition proved one's worth. She was blind to the fact that not being able to cherish and appreciate a quiet person, a hurting person, or a less-than-gifted person betrays a serious lack of character.

It was by means of a Good Friday "Through the Steps with Jesus" program at her church that Julie's heart was awakened. Walking through a room that depicted many of the stages of Passion Week helped her understand the depths of Christ's sacrifice. Sitting in a darkened sanctuary, she saw the true source of her acceptance—and in that light, she saw her inability to appreciate her husband and son as a sin. She saw herself passing on the sin of her father by making her daughters earn her love. When she got to the station where participants write down their sins and nail them to the cross, something inside Julie broke.

She wept. All those years of trying to earn something that Jesus had already bought. All those years of putting her daughters on the same treadmill that had made her own childhood feel like a never-ending hamster wheel. When she read the words "it is finished," uttered by Christ on the cross, she finally got the "finished" part. There was nothing more for her to do. Which meant there was nothing more for her husband to do. There was nothing more for her son, Brent, to do.

Acceptance reigns.

Cherishing could begin.

A New Message

Much of early Greek philosophy viewed mercy and compassion as weaknesses. Merciful people were considered overly sentimental and soft. Jesus came as the living embodiment of compassion and mercy, forever setting a new standard of what maturity and strength really are.

The cross looked like a defeat to much of the first-century world, even though it was the greatest victory ever won.

Jesus was different.

For starters, he taught a life of dependence: "Very truly I tell you," said Jesus, "the Son can do nothing by himself; he can only do what he sees his Father doing" (John 5:19). And to us, Jesus said, "If you remain in me and I in you, you will bear much fruit; apart from me you can do nothing" (John 15:5).

Jesus lived a life of compassion. About Jesus, Mark wrote, "He had compassion on them, because they were like sheep without a shepherd" (Mark 6:34).

In response to criticism from the Pharisees, Jesus proclaimed the superiority of mercy: "I desire mercy, not sacrifice" (Matthew 9:13).

Jesus made the gospel of mercy and grace the standard for relationships. We have to depend on God to receive grace every day, for his grace births compassion, and compassion compels us toward mercy.

We never stop being dependent. The moment we see ourselves as spiritually autonomous, we lose compassion, and when we lose compassion, we lose mercy. When we lose mercy, we lose the ability to keep cherishing an imperfect spouse.

This is a mental war. "Be transformed by the renewing of your mind," writes the apostle Paul (Romans 12:2). That's why we have to remind ourselves of the gospel every day—often many times a day.

Paying My Debt

The parable of a man forgiven a large debt who then imprisoned a man who owed him a small debt tells us two things: (1) we can't repay our own debts, but (2) once God pays our debts, we're to forgive others.

We receive grace and then we give grace.

More than being a duty, though, gospel truth is the doorway to what is truly a *glorious* life. It lifts our marriages to an entirely new level. Paul describes the glory of what we could call a "gospel marriage" in Titus 3. And trust me, this is the kind of marriage you want.

Paul paints a picture of what cherishing looks like and what it doesn't look like. It's a stark contrast. In context, this is not specifically addressing marriage and family life, but it's a fair application to read it with family in mind:

Remind them to be . . . ready for every good work, to speak evil of no one, to avoid quarreling, to be gentle, and to show every courtesy to everyone. For we ourselves were once foolish, disobedient, led astray, slaves to various passions and pleasures, passing our days in malice and envy, despicable, hating one another. But when the goodness and loving kindness of God our Savior appeared, he saved us, not because of any works of righteousness that we had done, but according to his mercy, through the water of rebirth and renewal by the Holy Spirit. This Spirit he poured out on us richly through Jesus Christ our Savior, so that, having been justified by his grace, we might become heirs according to the hope of eternal life. The saying is sure.

Titus 3:1–8 NRSV

The power to cherish begins with understanding the gospel message of "the goodness and loving kindness of God our Savior," who saved us "not because of any works of righteousness that we had done, but according to his mercy," and who has given us "renewal by the Holy Spirit."

But a key second part to the gospel is often left out. According to 2 Corinthians 5:15 (italics added), it's this: "And he died for all, *that* those who live should no longer live for themselves but for him who died for them and was raised again."

The gospel isn't just about being pardoned; it's also about being given a new life and learning to live with a new motivation, furthering the work Christ has begun in remaking the world—that's what we could call the "applied cherishing" part. It is inconceivable to Paul and the biblical writers that we could receive new life and the presence of the Holy Spirit but continue to live as we used to, with the same selfish motivations, trivial preoccupations, and tendency toward selfishness and evil.

Get Cherish to Give Cherish

The application of the gospel is this: "We love because he first loved us" (1 John 4:19). Another way to put this is that *we have to worship before we can work*. There's no other way. To stop worshiping is the spiritual equivalent of holding our breath. We will become weak and then desperate, sooner rather than later. Worshiping God—remembering his grace, remembering King Jesus, remembering the glory out of which we are called to live—changes us, recharges us, motivates us, transforms us. There can be no solid work—inside or outside marriage—without worship. There will be no long-term cherishing of our spouses until we are first cherished by God.

For us to love the way the Bible tells us to love means we can't go twenty-four hours without checking in with God to be loved, accepted, and affirmed, or else we'll run out of our own love to give. It's impossible to store up God's love, as life and relationships continually drain us. We need to learn to let God's cherishing presence continually flow through us. When Paul tells us in Ephesians 5:18 to be "filled with the Spirit," the original language is along the lines of "let yourself be continually filled with the Spirit." It's a command to let God keep filling us up with himself on an ongoing basis. More than this being an "imitation" of Christ, it's participation in the ongoing, life-giving grace of Christ.

In other words, as soon as we start living on our own, trying to cherish on our own, we turn off the engine of cherish and start to coast. It's only a matter of time until we stop.

Why is remembering the gospel so important for my continuing to cherish my spouse? It helps me remember that if God can cherish and delight in me, with all my weaknesses, insecurities, sins and hang-ups, the bar to be "cherish-worthy" is pretty much lying on the ground. When I honestly consider how irritating it would be for anyone but God to have the same patient conversations with me over and over, and yet never making me feel like I'm a bother, my thoughts about everyone else take on a different tone.

Julie hasn't yet nailed her paper confession to the cross in that church. She *mentally* nailed it there, but she kept the actual paper as a daily reminder. She wanted something tangible so she didn't forget the gospel.

Looking at that paper inside her Bible reminds her every day what God has forgiven her for, the source of her acceptance, and the debt she owes him. She does intend to nail the paper to the cross at next year's Passion Week, when the church holds the same ceremony.

Here's what Julie now understands: if you are in Christ, accepted by God, loved by God, cherished by God, forgiven by grace, and empowered by the Holy Spirit, then you'll understand the life-changing truth that *the God who cherishes the imperfect you is more than capable of helping you cherish an imperfect spouse.*

What It Looks Like

Once the gospel is accepted and is being lived out, Titus 3 tells us what life looks like. This is marriage at its highest and best. It is a marriage that shines and sparkles—one where cherishing and being cherished are showcased.

We are told first "to be ready for every good work, to speak evil of no one, to avoid quarreling, to be gentle, and to show every courtesy to everyone" (Titus 3:1–2).

Gospel people who have been cherished by God live like this:

- They are ready—eager, primed, zealous—for every good work.
- They speak evil of no one.
- They especially avoid quarreling (given that their call is reconciliation).
- They are gentle toward the faults of others, as God has been and continues to be gentle with them.
- They show every courtesy.

When you feel cherished by God, it follows that you want to cherish others, and the above list is part of what that means. Paul says that being cherished by God launches us on a nearly obsessive pursuit to do good works. In Titus 3:1–14 (NRSV) alone, Paul mentions this pursuit *three times*: "be ready for every good work" (verse 1), "devote themselves to good works" (verse 8), and "learn to devote themselves to good works" (verse 14).

Paul is *very* into good works proceeding out of grace.

So in a Christian marriage that seeks to cherish, husband and wife are *ready* for every good work. They are looking for ways to bless each other. No one speaks evil of anyone else, and since they are ready to do every good work, there is no *quarreling*. That's because they are *gentle* with each other and *show courtesy* to each other (Titus 3:2).

Before you think I've lost my mind and live on Mars ("come on, Gary, who lives like this?"), pause and ask, "Who *wouldn't* want to live in a family like this?"

"But how is it possible?"

Not just by deciding you really, really want to do it, but by choosing every day to preach the gospel to yourself and then to remind yourself, "This is our standard. Not just by avoiding being mean or harsh or not speaking ill of each other, but by daily reminding ourselves of how kind and good God has been to us, spending time with God to be daily renewed by the Holy Spirit so we can supernaturally forgive each other, treat each other gently, and actively look for good works to do to bless each other."

It sounds like a simple formula, but it's a powerful one: preach the gospel to yourself (receive God's favor) and then live out the gospel (express God's favor to others). That's the power to cherish—believing and receiving the gospel in which we are cherished beyond all measure and then living out the implications to cherish each other.

You will fail multiple times, but the wonderful thing about the gospel is that when you fail, you receive grace for yourself as much as you offer it to your spouse when they fail. It's not a pressurized performance, but rather it's a daily drawing down the freedom to gradually grow into the people we've always wanted to be— gracious, kind, forgiving, and enthusiastic about our spouses.

Julie started asking God for ways to do good works for Jeff. One afternoon he came in from doing some yard work, and she handed him a gift certificate for three professional massages. "You work so hard, honey. Maybe this will help you feel better."

Jeff had never had a professional massage before. Julie tended to be tight with the budget and always seemed to make Jeff feel like he had to sacrifice since he didn't earn as much money as other husbands did. Spending money on an indulgence that was just for him was something she had never done, as it might have communicated that she was okay with his lack of ambition. She saw how she had essentially been making Jeff pay for not earning more.

Instead of making Jeff pay, she wanted to bless him.

Jeff was speechless. When Julie saw how moved he was, she understood just how selfish and judgmental she had been. The unspoken message was always "you're not measuring up." Expressing a practical "thank you for being who you are" ministered to Jeff's soul in a way that surprised her.

It became infectious. Julie looked for new ways to spend money on Jeff, and when she did, she discovered she liked him a whole lot more. Cherishing had changed her heart.

In a way, Julie was cherishing her husband for perhaps the first time since they'd gotten married. Yes, she had always *loved* him. Jeff knew that. But now Julie was *cherishing* him. And they've never had a happier season of marriage.

In your marriage, are you careful to devote yourself to do good works for your spouse? Without this positive focus on doing good works, the goal of married life becomes not doing bad works, but that's not good enough. That's not cherishing; that's being a Pharisee ("I won't do bad things to you so you won't do bad things to me").

Are you actively looking every day for ways first to receive God's kindness and goodness, to be newly filled with the Spirit, and then to come home with an attitude of "God, please show me how to bless my spouse today. Help me find at least one good work to do at home." Are you receiving the gospel so powerfully that you feel compelled to find good works to do to bless your spouse on a regular basis?

Here's what it comes down to: *faith produces fruit.* If you're not concerned with how to show good works to your spouse, you have forgotten the way God has blessed you, the kindness of God, the goodness of God, the empowering of God through

Cherish

the Holy Spirit. So you've got to build up your faith in order to get the fruit.*

I know some of this may sound idealistic. I won't even pretend to say I've mastered this. But why wouldn't we want this? Doesn't it sound lovely? And if God offers it as an instruction, dare we say it's too lofty to shoot for?

What's the alternative? Going back to Titus 3, we see the alternative is what we *were*: "For we ourselves were once foolish, disobedient, led astray, slaves to various passions and pleasures, passing our days in malice and envy, despicable, hating one another" (Titus 3:3 NRSV). That's life apart from the gospel. Instead of being motivated by a glorious, eternal plan based on being loved and loving in return, we spend our days in trivial, selfish, self-absorbed pursuits.

The NIV translates this last phrase in verse 3 as "being hated and hating one another." I see a lot of marriages that fall into that trap. The root issue is they have started to hate their spouse and be hated by them. They think the issue is wet towels on the floor, not enough money, too much or too little sex, or something else. It's actually *spiritual rot*. They have forgotten the gospel. They aren't being cherished and cherishing; they aren't being loved and loving. They're just spending their days immersed in hatred. Until they go back to gospel living— preaching the gospel to themselves, receiving it, and living it out—they won't resolve the real issue.

---

* My book *Sacred Pathways* (rev. ed.; Grand Rapids: Zondervan, 2010) has been used by many churches to help people understand the best way for them to connect with God on a daily basis. It lists nine different "spiritual temperaments" so people can develop a devotional time uniquely suited to the disposition with which they were created by God. If you feel stunted in your devotional times, consider checking out the teaching there.

222

A life of being loved and loving is our spiritual inheritance. We don't have to hate each other.

The gospel gave Julie and Jeff a new marriage. It can do the same for you. Claim the life of being loved and loving. Preach the gospel to yourself every day, and then live it out every moment. That's the power behind cherish.

CHERISHING CHERISH

- To maintain motivation to cherish our spouses we need to remember how much we've been forgiven, what we've been saved from, and the price Christ paid to give us a second chance.

- Understanding the gospel—and reminding ourselves of the gospel—puts us in the mind-set and spiritual condition to keep on cherishing each other. Because Christ served me, I now serve you.

- To cherish each other in the way the Bible calls us to, we have to first receive and embrace the goodness and loving kindness of God, throw ourselves on his mercy, and be renewed by the Holy Spirit.

- The God who cherishes the imperfect you is more than capable of helping you cherish an imperfect spouse.

- Gospel marriages are ready to do good works for each other; they speak no evil of each other; they avoid quarreling and are gentle with each other; they show every courtesy.

- Without the gospel, many couples end up being hated and hating each other instead of being loved and loving each other.

QUESTIONS FOR
DISCUSSION AND REFLECTION

1. Did you feel accepted as a child? If so (or if not), how did it impact the way you look at God? How has it impacted the way you treat your spouse?

2. Discuss in your own words what God has saved you from. Confess what you truly deserve, given all that you were and have done.

3. Remember and describe the joy you experienced when Christ lifted that spiritual burden off your shoulders. What has salvation come to mean to you?

4. How do you feel most loved by God? What can you do in your devotional times to remember and receive his grace, affirmation, and comfort and to cultivate his presence and voice?

5. List two or three good works you can do for your spouse in the coming week.

6. When you review the fruit of the gospel, where are you strongest and where are you weakest?

- being zealous for good works
- never speaking evil of each other
- avoiding quarreling
- showing gentleness with each other
- showing each other every courtesy

Epilogue

My friend Dr. Greg Bledsoe was a junior medical student in a family practice clinic.[27] It was a typical day, and Greg was doing what medical students are supposed to do—"feign interest in the clinic's goings-on and try not to get in the way."

Eventually, Greg and the resident doctor walked into the room of an elderly female patient and her husband. The patient was close to eighty years old and sitting in a wheelchair. Her limbs had shrunk from a neuromuscular disease, and she sat tilted to the side with her mouth agape, drooling.

Greg noted the "spry energy of her spouse. He was alert, mentally sharp, even loquacious. He was equal to his feeble wife in age but in far better health. I was surprised because so often it is the other way around. We men tend to go downhill much more quickly than women, so usually it's a feeble husband being cared for by his healthy wife."

Greg felt an emotional and spiritual disease common to a young man—one who doesn't yet understand true love: "I must confess—I felt sorry for this husband."

The husband seemed to be in good spirits, even while wiping the drool off his wife's chin. Knowing the around-the-clock care such patients require, Greg also knew the exhausting demands placed on her caregiver. He glanced at her records and saw she still lived at home with him.

Her husband was that caregiver.

Please, God, not me, ever, Greg thought, as most young men would.

The resident physician was paged, and he stepped into the hall to answer it, leaving Greg alone in the clinic exam room with this patient and her husband.

"It was a bit awkward," Greg confesses. "At this point in my medical training I was basically an observer, so there was nothing I could contribute to the patient's medical care on my own. With my resident out in the hall, the clinic visit had come to a halt, and the patient's husband and I were left sitting together in the presence of his drooling and occasionally moaning wife, with nothing more to do than make polite small talk."

The awkwardness was broken by an enthusiastic exclamation from the husband. "She's my fishing buddy, you know," he said.

"I'm sorry?"

"She's my fishing buddy. Me and her have fished all over," he said.

"Really?"

"Yep. We used to set trotlines in the lake over there and get up every morning to check them," he replied, "We've been married more than fifty years."

Greg stared at the man whose eyes were sparkling, his mouth wide in a jovial, somewhat toothless grin.

He was *beaming*.

"Yessir, this one here's my fishing buddy," he said again, as he gently took her hand and affectionately smiled in her direction.

Greg reflects, "For the next ten minutes, I was transfixed as this man, who moments before I was pitying, regaled me with story after story of his life together with his wife. It was incredible. What was even more incredible, however, was the change that occurred in me.

"Watching this elderly man caress his wife's hand, kiss her cheek, wipe away her drool, and joyfully recount their lives together provoked a powerful transformation of perspective within me. Gone was any semblance of pity. Instead, in its place was . . . envy."

This senior citizen *cherished* his drooling, mentally absent, severely wrinkled elderly wife, and a much younger doctor, still single, *envied* the way this older man looked at and talked about his octogenarian wife.

The husband Greg talked to is certainly dead by now. He'll never know that his act of cherishing is going to be read by many. A few years after this encounter, Greg married a stunningly beautiful blonde still in her twenties with flawless skin and perfect muscle tone, but Greg realized those things don't define love, and they certainly don't sustain love.

You can cherish an eighty-something, wheelchair-bound, moaning and drooling "fishing buddy."

Cherish is built and sustained by a lifetime of choices reinforced over decades, so that someone becomes increasingly important to us because they always have been and they always will be. Many decades ago, the patient's husband likely laughed as he wiped a dab of ice cream off his date's mouth when they were in their twenties, and it feels no different to him to wipe a little drool off her chin now that she's his wife and in her eighties. It's the same woman, and he adores her. She's his Eve, and he can't even imagine—and wouldn't want to—being with someone else: "My dove, my perfect one, is the only one" (Song of Songs 6:9 ESV).

Cherish

If it pleases God, may this book multiply such stories until his church is filled with husbands who deeply cherish their wives and wives who eagerly and generously cherish their husbands until the very end.

Notes

1. Quoted in Arlene Croce, "Balanchine Said," *New Yorker* (January 26, 2009), www.newyorker.com/magazine/2009/01/26/balanchine-said (accessed April 11, 2016).

2. Ibid.

3. Sarah Jessica Parker, exec. producer, "City Ballet: Partnering," S1 E9 (November 3, 2013), http://tinyurl.com/n7lusu9 (accessed April 11, 2016).

4. I've seen this quote in several places. This particular wording is taken from Dennis and Barbara Rainey, *The New Building Your Mate's Self-Esteem* (Nashville: Nelson, 1995), 268.

5. Tyler Ward, *Marriage Rebranded: Modern Misconceptions and the Unnatural Art of Loving Another Person* (Chicago: Moody, 2014), 91.

6. Quoted in Marriage Missions International, "Quotes on 'Communication Tools,'" http://marriagemissions.com/about-us-2/quotes-on-communication-tools/ (accessed April 11, 2016).

7. Nicole Johnson, *The Invisible Woman: A Special Story of Mothers* (Nashville: Nelson, 2005).

8. Emily Esfahani Smith, "Masters of Love," *The Atlantic*, June 12, 2014, www.theatlantic.com/health/archive/2014/06/happily-ever-after/372573 (accessed April 11, 2016).

9. The Gottman Institute, "Research FAQs: What Are the Negative Behavior Patterns That Can Predict Divorce," www.gottman.com/about/research/faq (accessed April 11, 2016).

10. Cited in Paul Kengor, "The Untold Story of How Nancy Reagan Would Have Taken a Bullet for Her Husband," www.foxnews.com/opinion/2016/03/07/untold-story-how-nancy-reagan-would-have-taken-bullet-for-her-husband.html (accessed May 31, 2016).

11. N. T. Wright, *Reflecting the Glory: Meditations for Living Christ's Life in the World* (Minneapolis: Augsburg, 1998), 64.

12. Smith, "Masters of Love."

13. "Gratitude Basics: The Benefits of Gratitude," *Psychology Today*, www.psychologytoday/basics/gratitude (accessed April 11, 2016).

14. See Smith, "Masters of Love."

15. Rainey, *The New Building Your Mate's Self-Esteem*, 29–37. I very slightly amended their list.

16. Ibid., 110.

17. See, e.g., Bill and Pam Farrel, *The Secret Language of Successful Couples: The Keys for Unlocking Love* (Eugene, OR: Harvest House, 2009), 25, 120–21, 130.

18. Dietrich Bonhoeffer, *Life Together* (New York: Harper & Row, 1954), 97.

19. John Chrysostom, "Homily XX on Ephesians," quoted in *Marriage: An Orthodox Perspective*, 3rd rev. ed., John Meyendorff (Crestwood, NY: St. Vladimir's Seminary Press, 1984), 89–90.

20. Rainey, *The New Building Your Mate's Self-Esteem*, 116.

21. Ibid., 117.

22. Sam Crabtree, *Practicing Affirmation: God-Centered Praise of Those Who Are Not God* (Wheaton, IL: Crossway, 2011), 7.

23. Quoted in Michelle Trudeau, "Human Connections Start with a Friendly Touch," September 20, 2010, www.npr.org/templates/story/story.php?storyId=128795325 (accessed April 21, 2016).

24. San Francisco State University, "Buying Experiences, Not Possessions, Leads to Greater Happiness," *Science Daily*, February 17, 2009, www.sciencedaily.com/releases/2009/02/090207150518.htm (accessed April 21, 2016).

25. Tim Keller, *The Meaning of Marriage: Facing the Complexities of Commitment with the Wisdom of God* (New York: Riverhead, 2011), 153.

26. N. T. Wright, *The Challenge of Jesus: Rediscovering Who Jesus Was and Is* (Downers Grove, IL: InterVarsity, 1999), 186.

27. This section is based on a blog post Greg Bledsoe graciously allowed to be posted on my blog at www.garythomas.com. I'm putting the words in third person instead of first to be consistent with the rest of the book, but this entire section is based on what Greg wrote in his own words. He has been published in numerous medical journals and blogs regularly at ghbledsoe.com.

Contacting Gary

Although Gary enjoys hearing from readers, it is neither prudent nor possible for him to offer counsel via email, mail, Facebook, or other social media. Thanks for your understanding.

Website:
www.garythomas.com
Blog:
www.garythomas.com/blog
Twitter:
@garyLthomas
Facebook
www.facebook.com/authorgarythomas

To book Gary for a speaking event, please contact him through his website or email alli@garythomas.com.

Every Good Marriage Begins with a Funeral

Gary Thomas

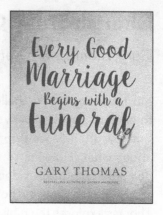

An authentic marriage begins here.

The journey toward authenticity in your marriage starts in the last place you'd think. Sign up today to receive Gary's free ebook *Every Good Marriage Begins with a Funeral*: www.garythomas .com/everygoodmarriage.

Cherish Study Guide with DVD

Gary Thomas with Beth Graybill

Most marriage books challenge us to explore a biblical view of love. But how often do we stop to think about what it means to cherish one another? In this video-based study, bestselling author Gary Thomas explores the biblical view of what it means to cherish. You will be challenged to take your love to a new level by learning what it means to truly cherish your spouse.

Session titles include:

Session 1: To Love and to Cherish
Session 2: Your Honor
Session 3: The Art of Cherishing Your Spouse
Session 4: Cherishing Your Unique Spouse
Session 5: This Is How Your Spouse Stumbles
Session 6: Keep on Cherishing

The videos, discussions, and activities will help you discover a new way of relating to your spouse, so that you are not only open to God's love but also start letting it change you from the inside out.

This pack contains one study guide and one DVD in an Amaray case.

Available in stores and online!

Sacred Marriage

What If God Designed Marriage to Make Us Holy More Than to Make Us Happy?

Gary Thomas

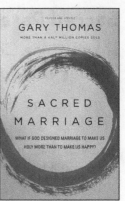

Your marriage is more than a sacred covenant with another person.

It is a spiritual discipline designed to help you know God better, trust him more fully, and love him more dearly. Gary Thomas's *Sacred Marriage* has attained the rank of a contemporary classic. This revised edition has been streamlined to be a faster read without losing the depth that so many readers have valued. And it may very well profoundly alter the contours of your marriage.

Sacred Marriage doesn't tell how to build a better marriage; it shows how your marriage can help you deepen your relationship with God. From the practice of forgiveness, to the ecstasy of lovemaking, to the history you and your spouse create together, everything about your marriage is filled with the potential for discovering and revealing Christ's character.

With provocative discussion questions for couples and small groups, this book will most certainly change you. Because whether it is delightful or difficult, your marriage can become a doorway to a closer walk with God.

Available in stores and online!

Sacred Parenting

How Raising Children Shapes Our Souls

Gary Thomas

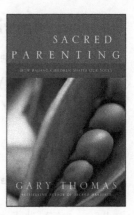

Parenting is a school for spiritual formation—and our children are our teachers.

The journey of caring for, rearing, training, and loving our children will profoundly alter us forever.

Sacred Parenting is unlike any other parenting book you have ever read. This is not a how-to book that teaches you ways to discipline your kids or help them achieve their full potential. Instead of discussing how parents can change their kids, *Sacred Parenting* turns the tables and demonstrates how God uses our kids to change us.

You've read all the method books. Now take a step back and receive some much-needed inspiration. You'll be encouraged by stories that tell how other parents handled the challenges and difficulties of being a parent—and how their children transformed their relationship with God. *Sacred Parenting* affirms the spiritual value of being a parent, showing you the holy potential of the parent-child relationship.

Available in stores and online!

Sacred Influence

How God Uses Wives to Shape the Souls of Their Husbands

Gary Thomas

God calls women to influence and move their husbands in positive ways.

If you're sick of all the ways you've tried to bring about change in your marriage—the silent treatment, nagging, one-way discussions, or pleading—it's time to set aside those broken methods for a Christ-based approach. This book demonstrates how women can inspire, influence, and help their husbands move in positive directions. Replacing your plan of action with God's leads to a marital transformation where both partners are moving in sync, the way God intended.

Gary Thomas draws concepts from his bestseller, *Sacred Marriage*, and outlines practical applications you can start using today. He also shows how marriages were transformed through these methods employed by real-life women.

In these pages, you'll also find a fresh perspective to help you understand your husband: the view of the marriage relationship through a man's eyes. Thomas gives you insider information on how men think, feel, and can truly be motivated.

Available in stores and online!

"Cherish is full of wisdom, practical advice, and candor on a subject so personal and sacred—how to live the marriage you want every day. Gary brings truth and reminds us of Jesus in the midst of our earthly relationships."
—JENNIE ALLEN, founder of IF:GATHERING

"My dove, my perfect one, is the only one."
Song of Songs 6:9 ESV

Every man and woman wants to be cherished by their spouse.
Here's how a couple can make that happen.

When a husband and wife know they are cherished by their spouse, it brings out the best in both of them.

Millions of couples pledge "to love and to cherish" each other on their wedding day, so why is there so much talk about love in marriage but not about what it means to cherish?

Bestselling author Gary Thomas believes that discovering how to better cherish your spouse has the power to infuse your relationship with new hope and promise. His earlier groundbreaking book, *Sacred Marriage*, changed the way husbands and wives thought about God's purpose for marriage. Now, he goes beyond love to explore how to create a *cherishing* marriage.

- Understand how you as a husband or wife can shape your mind and heart to treasure your spouse above all other men or women in the world.
- Learn how to remove the obstacles that keep you from holding your spouse in the highest regard.
- Discover the practical act of "showcasing" your spouse, which helps them thrive even as it increases your own affection for them.
- Husbands will be challenged to no longer make their wives feel "invisible," but rather honored, seen, and adored.
- Learn how to draw on God's empowering presence and truth to delight in your spouse as God delights in you.

Fill your relationship with new hope and promise.

Unleash the power of cherish in your marriage.

GARY THOMAS is a writer-in-residence who also serves on the teaching team at Second Baptist Church in Houston, Texas, and the author of eighteen books, including the bestselling *Sacred Marriage*, that have sold more than a million copies worldwide and have been translated into a dozen languages. He and his wife, Lisa, have been married for thirty years.

RELIGION / Christian Living / Love & Marriage
USD $14.99 / CAD $18.50
ISBN 978-0-310-34729-3

51499

Cover design: James W. Hall IV

ZONDERVAN®
.com

9 780310 347293